Competitive Running

How to advance from casual running to practicing a competitive sport

by

Dr. Alexander Gentemann

This book reflects the personal experiences of the author. Any advice within should therefore be considered from the reader's perspective first. It is possible that individual reactions to training concepts or single pieces of advice vary from reader to reader. Every runner should undergo regular checkups by trained medical personnel to exclude physical restraints or undergo professional treatment. Every aspect of this book serves as suggestions that need to be evaluated under the condition of the individual runner's body. The author rejects all negative effects or injuries resulting from following the recommendations presented in this book.

This ebook is licensed for your personal enjoyment only. This ebook may not be re-sold or given away to other people. If you like to share this book with another person, please purchase an additional copy for each person you share it with.

Copyright © 2016 Alexander Gentemann. All rights reserved. Including the right to reproduce this book or portions thereof, in any form. No part of this text may be reproduced in any form without the express written permission of the author.

Version 2017.07.25

Table of Content

Foreword..1
1. Introduction..3
   1.1 The starting point.......................................4
   1.2 The conventional approach.......................5
   1.3 Setting a personal goal..............................6
   1.4 How to improve?..7

2 The Columns of Training..................................9
   2.1 The training paces and how they relate to heart rate.........10
      2.1.1 Resting heart rate.............................11
      2.1.2 Heart Rate Zones.............................13
      2.1.3 Respiratory threshold.......................15
      2.1.4 Heart Rate Training vs. Pace Based Training............16
      2.1.5 Pace based training for interval running...................19

3. Developing the Columns................................21
   3.1 The column of endurance.........................22
      3.1.1 The two basic philosophies of endurance running....22
      3.1.2 Easy and recovery running................24
      3.1.3 Endurance running............................25
      3.1.4 Lactate Threshold Running................27
      3.1.5 The long run.....................................33
   3.2 The column of power.................................36
   3.3 The column of speed.................................41

3.3.1 Neuromuscular training..41

3.3.2 Lactate tolerance training...42

3.4.3 The maximum number of intervals............................45

3.4. The column of running form and holding strength..........47

3.4.1. Form adjustments as a warning sign........................49

3.4.2 Training for running form..51

3.4.3 Stability exercises to improve form deterioration......53

3.4.4 Muscle exercises to overcome stability issues...........56

4. Periodization of training...58
4.1 The weekly training cycle..58

4.2 Monthly training cycles...64

4.3 The base cycle..65

4.4 The build cycle...76

4.5 Example training cycles different athletes train by......84

4.6 The peak and race cycles...93

4.6.1 The 5K prep/race cycle..97

4.6.2 The 10K prep cycle..101

4.6.3 The half marathon prep/race cycle.........................105

4.6.4 The marathon prep/race cycle...............................109

4.7 Periodization across a season.....................................123

5 Design of a monthly cycle..124

5.1 Time spend running during training week.................125

5.2 The connection between training time and number of sessions per week..128

5.3 Designing the monthly training cycle........................134

5.4 How to put it all together?..141

   5.4.1 Training goals..143

   5.4.2 Improving the base..143

   5.4.3 Improving lactate threshold level..................147

   5.4.4 The cycle of improvement.............................150

   5.4.5 Training plan adjustments..............................152

   5.4.6 Example of 5K plan including adjustments...155

5.5 Alternative Race Cycle for two weeks before race.........160

5.6 Improvement throughout the cycle..............................162

6. Racing...166
7. Recovery..171
   7.1 Different recovery methods under ordinary conditions...171

     7.1.1 Short term recovery after every run..............174

     7.1.3 Active recovery..175

     7.1.3 Passive Recovery...176

   7.2 Injury and how prevention works...............................178

8. Bicycle cross training...181
   8.1 Heart rate based training...181

   8.2 Cross training approaches..183

     8.2.1 Cross training to overcome fatigue................183

    8.2.2 Cross training to overcome injury............................187

8. Appendix..190

Foreword

Note (concerning the ebook version): make sure to switch on the feature to update books with the latest version in your amazon account to receive regular updates on this book.

For many people running is an enjoyable hobby they practice to relax after work and to stay fit. For many it also turns into a competitive sport, the possibility to challenge oneself and to compete against others. Often times this evolution leads to a journey of improvement, the understanding of the training process: how does one become a faster runner? On this journey, websites are reviewed, books are bought and training plans executed. Many runners realize that a vast portion of the available running literature is geared towards the absolute beginner. These books deal with aspects like what a proper running shoe should look like or how to use running as a means to fight obesity. On the other hand, fewer books exist that are written by successful coaches of world class athletes. Many aspects of daily training are implied in these advanced publications that are not necessarily known to a runner who has understood the beginners' books but does not have access to world class coaching. Therefore, it is quite difficult to advance from the status of a beginner towards the competitive running environment. Many runners will never advance enough using the training plans they are accustomed to to fully utilize the training concepts of these advanced books. Other runners will simply get injured on the way by taking the wrong approach or simply by doing too much.

For the runner who wishes to improve beyond the beginner status, triggered by a personal need of the author, this book was written. This type of runner's questions how to advance past the rookie's running methods will be addressed. Also, how to approach this journey without getting injured is of great importance. This advancement process also implies to have fun along the way. A lot of runners feel that competitiveness is synonymous with a reduction in or even the removal of the joy of running. It will be shown that the idea of becoming a better runner, and thereby being able to compete well in races, is merely dependent on consistency and the right planning, not simply by training harder. To take this concept to a greater level, a method is introduced how to race well with enjoyment as the key element.

In summary, the purpose of this book is to close the gap between beginners' literature and books written by and for professional coaches.

1. Introduction

A few years ago I was looking for an endurance sport that I could conveniently practice besides work even though I had to travel quite a bit. Naturally, running was high on my list and I started by running three times a week at a somewhat taxing pace, always the same 10K route and the same pace. I did not have a training plan or even thought I needed one. I happened to improve (faster pace at the same effort) for about three month until I consistently ran that 10K round at about 45min. Somehow I was never able to run any faster after that, I tried, I failed. On top of that, I was getting tired of the same workout routine that took place almost every other day. So I started to ask myself the question: "How can I run faster while having more fun at the same time?". And is both even possible in combination?

So I started to look for literature on the subject, read more than a few books, and began following the advice prescribed by the authors. But somehow nobody seemed to have written a book for the ambitious hobby runner with a mediocre time slower than 40min (10K) who wanted to improve. I found a lot of beginners books and a few geared towards people who wanted to improve based on a 33min 10K time. So I began my journey of finding out what really did work for those like myself who are stuck in the middle. I followed a lot of advice from books and people, made many mistakes (which I paid for dearly in races) and learned theories of why and how the human body can adapt to training. I arrived at an easy to adopt process that helps any runner improve their personal best times from mile racing to the marathon.

This book describes that process along the path I was taking. The goal is to help the reader become a better runner (yes, this includes much more fun during every training run!). The book also focuses on avoiding most of the mistakes I made on the way.

1.1 The starting point

As mentioned above, my starting point of running three similar runs per week is probably very close to where a lot of other people also get stuck in their running. The pace that can be achieved at a given race distance is very individual and can vary with personal talent and prior training. Thus, whether you begin at 38min (10K) or 65min is not important. Key is that with training three times a week in the exact same way a runner will approach his personal natural speed in the given situation in his life. For an Olympic talent this may be a 33min 10K. Important is that the perceived effort will be about the same. A world class runner could run a 10K training run in 35min and it would be a slow run for him while most other people struggle with such a pace. Therefore, the slower your personal natural pace is in a given race the harder (because the longer) a runner is working. This describes the first problem with most running books: they talk about a certain distance that you train while really time at a certain pace is important (later more on that subject).

If you have reached the point where you get stuck at a certain pace with any weekly training ritual you have reached my starting point. From there, I tried out different training plans that I got from books or off the Internet and they seemed to work in some respects (e.g. ability to run for longer times) but I was maybe able to run a 44min 10K, not much faster. I followed a weekly training plan (every week the same) for about one year before upgrading to a monthly plan that again I kept repeating. Finally, I arrived at a plan that included periodization with three phases (base, build prep/race). The latter is what I will work out as the goal principle for this book and how to apply that principle to your individual needs.

1.2 The conventional approach

In conventional running books the author often uses the first part to introduce the physiological aspects of the human body that happen during physical activity. They introduce terms such as lactic acid, Vo2max and others. Instead of doing this, I will refer you to "The Science of Running" by Steve Magness which I have enjoyed much. The second part of running books often cover the authors personal training philosophy as well as key principles of training. Also, training plans are often introduced.

I found that many authors' starting point is a well trained runner who has been training for many years. A U.S. coach on the collegiate level may never encounter a mediocre runner in his life because from my perspective the college freshman with a running scholarship is already a great runner. They need different training from what I needed (and still need). Therefore, the presented concepts and training plans skip over the basics and represent the "icing on the cake". This caused a problem for me because in spite of following the given advice by world class coaches (e.g. "Run Faster" by Brad Hudson) I did not improve. It is not that these books are of minor quality. They are in fact outstanding from the perspective from which they were written. But they did only help me indirectly by presenting some of the concepts I am using today.

Also, the science (physiological) part of many books has little connection to the training principles (as pointed out by Steve Magness in "The Science of Running") simply because many training principles have not been scientifically studied. One example for this was the then popular HIIT (High intensity interval training) method that was only studied using a few untrained individuals. HIIT is, simply put, a set of short intervals at extremely high intensity with recovery time between them. On the tested untrained runners the method worked quite well (better than steady running for the control group) as they had sufficient recovery time between the workouts of the week and little prior exhaustion (due to little training before the study). But for well trained runners it turns out the method had little effect or even caused injury. Due to this lack of scientific evidence or ineffective studies it comes as little surprise that many coaches have differing training formulas (if often times only in details) that each have their merit in a certain scenario. Yet, nobody told me how I fit into this jungle of different approaches as well as sometimes outdated (or even anecdotal) principles.

What struck me was that in many books a certain run is introduced (say e.g. the long run) but not much detail is given as to the pace, heart rate or other aspects that I had no clue about. Starting at a set pace would make my heart rate increase and starting at a set heart rate would let my pace decline over time. So how to approach such a run? In very fast runs (such as lactic interval runs) heart rate information (although often used in literature to give indication how to run them) I found quite useless as the heart rate would not pick up quickly enough to present a difference. So what to do?

Through a lot of trial and error I found a system that I like to present in the following chapters.

1.3 Setting a personal goal

My starting point to trying to understand how faster running worked was a set goal. I thought running a 10K in under 40 minutes seemed reasonable enough. It also seemed to not be that far away. Starting out at 45min seemed close to 40min. Not diving into the discussion of how sensible such goals are many people have them, just like myself. The only problem with goals like that is that from what I learned at least they do not make a whole lot of sense.

The simple reason why this is the case is that too many variables have an effect on the actual time for a set distance. Also, a race (this maximum effort to be achieved on race day) happens only once in a while yet training happens on the majority of days of the week. Therefore, my goal shifted step by step towards more enjoyment of training runs and towards the celebration of different goals. Now, every individual has to define this for themselves but I take more out of a half marathon run these days at submaximum effort but achieving a personal best (faster pace) at a set heart rate while enjoying a landscape. I still improve my personal best for the 10K at the same time. It is just that at least for my own situation, 40min for the 10K was in fact quite far away from the starting point of a 45min time.

My journey through training principles generally lead to unnecessarily exhausting and painful training while not becoming a faster runner at the same time. Regardless of the personal goals an improvement can not be forced as it will happen gradually over time.

The other aspect of training is the focus on a specific distance. This has become very popular in recent years with training plans for most distances between the 1500m and the marathon. For a professional runner this would be natural as a set body has a set predisposition towards a certain race distance (due to muscle fiber composition and other genetically influenced aspects). These pro runners are probably at over 90% of their maximum given ability for all race distances in the mentioned spectrum. But I hardly believe that this is the case for an intermediate runner like myself. Once a runner improves his fitness he can safely assume he is able to run faster at all distances (given he actually trains for that distance). Back in the 1970s and before, world class athletes often times competed in the whole spectrum of distances on a high level with their times considerably better than most hobby runners today. Thus, as a hobby runner, I abandoned that fundamental thought very early. As I found that simply following a training plan off the Internet is not the worst thing a runner can do I also found that such training plans only represent the last four to twelve weeks before a race. But what is really important is what happens before a runner even starts such a plan. This is another focus of this book: where does the race specific plan actually fit in? How are these plans designed and what do I need?

1.4 How to improve?

The general concept in any aspect of life when it comes to improvement is doing something repeatedly that you are not used to and the specific skill will improve. In running, the principle of supercompensation is also an obvious fact of life and dominates everything a runner does during training. You exercise a skill beyond todays' ability and the body will react with preparation for the requested future level.

A specific ability needs to be stressed and the body will improve that ability over time. The real question is then: which abilities do you need to stress and how long does it take for the improvement? The first part of the question points towards the different types of training while the second part implies recovery time.

Most hobby runners know about different types of runs such as long or interval runs. But what are they actually good for? This in turn points towards the question: how should a certain type of run be carried out in order to be most effective? And what is there to avoid? Also, once this aspect is understood, when should I repeat a similar stress so the body keeps improving?

The answer to these questions are presented partially in literature and implicitly in all serious training plans off the Internet. Piecing together the information is what counts as one 'should train as little as possible to reach a given adaption' as Jack Daniels points out. This is where a lot of people's training goes off the rails. Doing the additional interval might not be beneficial and even hurt performance. Therefore, the complete picture needs to be studied.

To do this, we need to introduce the COLUMNS OF TRAINING, the basic abilities that a runner must improve to run at a set pace for a set time. After that we need to look at how often, intense and when they need to be stressed in order to trick the body into adaption. Generally, ADAPTION TAKES PLACE DURING RECOVERY, not during training.

2 The Columns of Training

As many authors point out: running is a series of small jumps of a certain rate (cadence) and distance for a given time. A slower runner is thus different from a faster runner because he can either not jump as far, as quickly or for such a long time. This quickly leads to the basic abilities a runner needs for speedy running.

Thinking of a house that needs to carry the roof the basic abilities could be looked at as columns that hold said roof. If any one of the columns is weak the runner will lack certain aspects in a race. As a consequence, the columns that represent the basic abilities of a runner also represent the basic aspects a runner needs to train. Important is that only if all columns keep improving the race times will improve up to the physiological limit. The columns of training are:

- Endurance
- Power
- Speed
- Running Form and (Holding) Strength

Endurance is the ability to run for a long time, power is needed to take long steps (or run up hills), speed is to turn over your legs quickly. Running form points to efficiency of running and (holding) strength to maintaining an efficient running form for an expected time.

Just by looking at race results and talking to athletes about the details of a race can often times resolve where an individual is held back. Examples are runners being able to run at low speeds for long periods of time (good endurance, low speed and/or power) or runners who are fatigued 100m before the finish line but can explode in a massive sprint at the end (low endurance, good speed). Someone might not have trouble when a race is hilly (good power) but falls behind during a race on a flat circuit (endurance and/or speed issue). From such examples it becomes clear that simply following a training plan will not be sufficient as training history and natural abilities are very important aspects. Training plans are therefore individual in nature.

In this context it means the status of development concerning the columns of training are different for every runner. In theory, maintaining the developed abilities and focusing on the weaknesses will result in short term improvements. The longer the training history and the more one-sided the training the more dramatic the improvements will be once training is shifted to address the weaknesses. I have witnessed 10K times improve from 42min to 38min in a matter of six months because all but one ability (power in this case) were well developed in a runner. A beginner of course has to work on all abilities step by step which will take time. The upside is that a runner will see small yet continuous improvements to different aspects of running once he knows what these aspects are.

2.1 The training paces and how they relate to heart rate

Now that we know about the columns of training, and before discussion them in detail, it is necessary to translate those basic abilities to the different ways to improve them. This is where heart rate and pace come into the picture. I read a couple of times that pro athletes rely on pace based training plans and often times do not even wear a heart rate monitor while they are running. I found that the longer I run the more I develop a feeling for the relationship between perceived effort and current heart rate during a run. That statement holds especially true for slower runs and it is one aspect of the evolution of a runner to be able to relate feeling of effort to actual heart rate. However, as one undertakes this journey it is most favorable in my opinion to rely on heart rate information for the majority of training runs. The assumption that just because a professional does something it must be good seldomly holds true. In fact, if one wants to act like a pro he needs to improve to the skill level of a pro.

2.1.1 Resting heart rate

Before the heart rates for training are discussed the resting heart rate needs to be addressed. While its absolute value is influenced by many factors such as training level and genetic predisposition it is of advantage to monitor this value on a regular basis. I use a heart rate monitor that measures heart rate around the clock and automatically presents the value in the morning for the previous night. One could also measure it every day while still in bed in the morning but I found this method to be too inaccurate and time consuming.

Two aspects are very important to a distance runner which can be related to resting heart rate: overtraining and illness affecting the heart-lung system. While overtraining of muscles, tendons and joints will be noticed through pain in the affected areas this statement does not hold true for heart, lungs and blood vessels. In order for the body to improve inflammation seems to play a role to direct e.g. muscle growth. Yet, this effect can get out of hand which is called overtraining syndrome. The runner experiences a decrease in performance even though he trains hard. While pro runners might want to approach the boundary of overtraining to maximize training efficiency it is advisable for the hobby athlete to stay away from it.

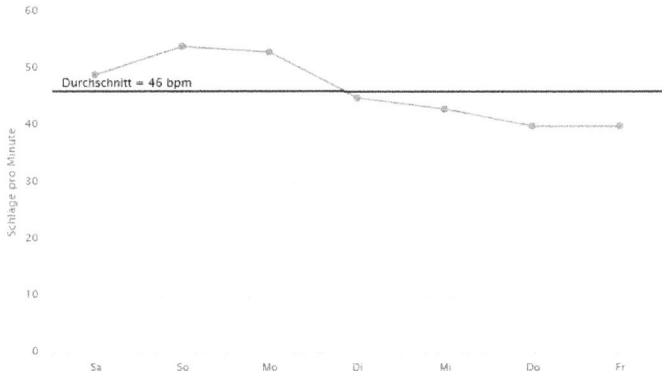

Fig 1: Example Resting Heart Rate. Head cold on Sat/Sun and following recovery without any training.

The resting heart rate, once recorded over a longer period of time, will present a possible warning signal (apart from performance loss and feeling not well of course) to adjust training. For example (fig. 1), the resting heart rate might consistently be at about 40 beats per minute over the course of a month while the runner is considerably rested during this period. Now, if the resting heart rate was increased above say 50 bpm one morning along with cold symptoms a runner can assume that his heart-lung system is affected. Training under such conditions may lead to severe inflammation of the heart muscle, a possibly fatal condition. Fig. 1 presents a method to estimate a time frame when training can be resumed. In this case, the athlete knows his normal resting heart rate (around 40bpm) which is again reached on Thursday. He will then resume training on Friday.

The other more common situation is overtraining. The symptom is again a raised resting heart rate. I set the threshold at about 10bpm increase over the long term average but this might be different for different people. During a period of hard training, most likely during a time of increased mileage, discriminating a normal feeling of exhaustion from overtraining can be done by looking at resting heart rate. If a runner detects an increase in resting heart rate during such a phase a couple of days of easy running is introduced into the training program at any stage until resting heart rate is back to normal. More often than not a runner will observe improved performance at the end of such an intervention. Complete rest in this situation does not help much as many runners feel flat after not training at all. But, if a runner ignores an elevated resting heart rate total rest for even a couple of months might be unavoidable.

2.1.2 Heart Rate Zones

Different concepts of heart rate zone training do exist. What all of them have in common is to divide the heart rate spectrum between rest and maximum heart rate into zones of different training purpose. In principle, I followed this system and I also tried different variations with varying success. In general, I found that programs geared towards novice runners tend to use lower heart rates for easy and long runs (which make up about 80% of running time). On the other hand, looking at pro runners publications e.g. on Strava, I found that they even run their easy runs at a brisk pace. The system on which I based my running system was then very close to what I found in Joel Friels book (Total heart rate training) which I recommend.

First, the lactate threshold (LT) heart rate, being the effort beyond which the body produces considerably more lactic acid than it can clear, is estimated. At paces beyond this point endurance running can not be sustained for more than a couple of minutes. First, LT needs to be determined via a test. The LT test is carried out as follows: according to Joe Friel and others an athlete runs an all-out 30min effort (I took a race effort over 7km at the time) and calculates the average heart rate of the final 20min. This will provide a good estimate of the lactate threshold heart rate. Based on this heart rate, say 168bpm, the training zones can be calculated using the tables in Friels book. One can now find a couple of calculators on the Internet (e.g. http://www.datacranker.com/heart-rate-zones/). For the given example of 168bpm the following heart rate zones result:

1 - Active Recovery	0 - 143
2 - Endurance	143 - 150
3 - Tempo	151 - 159
4 - Lactate Threshold	160 - 167
5a - Above Threshold	168 - 172
5b - Aerobic Capacity	173 - 178
5c - Anaerobic Capacity	178 <

Table 1. Heart Rate Zones (not adjusted)

As my maximum heart rate is 181bpm at this time (decreases with age) the values seem reasonable. The maximum heart rate HRmax is most easily found at the end of a 5K race with a hefty final sprint (you should be close to it when you cross the finish line). But I found that my lactate threshold runs sort of leveled off at around 163bpm. Also, most literature does not advise doing lactate threshold runs at more than 90% of maximum heart rate (90% x 181bpm – 163bpm). Additionally, since I use a running watch that estimates LT, 163bpm was presented to me once more (the watch data varies between 162bpm and 164bpm and at least in my case I can recommend using it). Therefore, I adjusted LT to 163bpm instead (remember the all-out running method really is an estimation). As the result, I received the following heart rate zones from the tables:

1 - Active Recovery	0 - 139
2 - Endurance	139 - 145
3 - Tempo	147 - 153
4 - Lactate Threshold	155 - 162
5a - Above Threshold	163 - 166
5b - Aerobic Capacity	168 - 173
5c - Anaerobic Capacity	173 <

Table 2. Heart Rate zones (adjusted)

Note that the adjusted zones still make little difference to the values before around the slower end of the spectrum. As a consequence, I do my recovery/easy running at around 136bpm (75% of max. heart rate) and my endurance runs at around 144bpm (80% of max. heart rate). This system results in considerably higher paces as many other systems in which recovery takes place sometimes below 65% of max. heart rate. Whether or not you choose to adjust the heart rate zones, it is often not a bad idea to stay a couple of bpm below the estimated LT HR as the training benefit is still present. From this discussion alone, the concept of intervals slightly above LT pace make a lot of sense. If those were run for say 10 minutes each lactic acid would accumulate in the blood stream and LT HR will be exceeded. Yet, if these intervals are kept shorter (say below 4 minutes each) sufficient oxygen will be present to convert lactic acid back to muscle fuel, the blood lactic acid level never increases significantly. From an LT perspective, the body learns to produce and quickly clear lactic acid which will improve LT pace while keeping LT HR (almost) constant.

2.1.3 Respiratory threshold

The boundary between endurance and tempo runs is defined by the respiratory (or aerobic) threshold. In terms of the example used above, at around 147bpm breathing becomes significantly harder for myself. Below this threshold a relaxed conversation is possible (more so in the easy running zone). For many runners, easy and endurance running means that a breathing pattern of three breaths in and three breaths out per step (in, in, in, out, out, out) is possible. Beyond the respiratory threshold, however, they are forced to switch to a two breaths in and two breaths out breathing pattern (in, in, out, out). The heart rate for this threshold is easily found by slowly increasing the speed from easy running pace on. The heart rate at which the breathing pattern needs to be shifted is the respiratory threshold. It should coincide with the lower tempo zone. This threshold can then be used to verify the heard rate zones established above. Remember the established zones are based on estimates for the lactate threshold not exact measurements.

Yet, since any physical process inside the body deals in equilibriae slowly changing with running pace it is not necessary to hit certain heart rates spot on. An endurance run is then done in a zone rather at a certain HR by adjusting running pace. In my case, I would aim for a heart rate of 144bpm which is slightly below the upper endurance HR limit. The main reason for this is that I like to keep a bit of distance to the respiratory threshold.

But how to get into the HR zone? I would find out the appropriate pace for my level of running by consulting the tables proposed by Jack Daniels (in detail below). For the current example of an easy run pace (e.g. 5:10min/km @ 136bpm) this would e.g. result in endurance run pace of around 4:58min/km @ 144bpm. I find these runs very useful especially when the respiratory threshold is approached from the lower end at the end of such runs. The example illustrates that any runner needs to know at least roughly which pace to begin HR based runs to ease into them and avoid pace fluctuations. In the following, the paces correlating with the individual heart rate zones will therefore be estimated.

2.1.4 Heart Rate Training vs. Pace Based Training

Now that the concept of HR training zones is introduced the question arises at which point pace information comes into play. I approach the subject from different angles. For easy runs, I estimate initial pace on the basis of runs I did before. E.g. a run on a standard route at e.g. 5:30min/km leads to a heart rate of 136bpm after one hour of running. So I might begin my run with an easy 5:15min/km and adjust to slower (or faster) pace after I have reached the 136bpm for this easy run. I do the same for endurance runs. This way, my average pace on a standard route reflects my training progress for easy and endurance running. This method is advised to apply for easy runs, endurance runs and lactate threshold runs where the appropriate heart rates (HR) will soon be well known to the runner. Then, train and monitor improvement at the same time by keeping HR constant and comparing average pace on a set course.

However, heart rate takes a while (in my case about 10-15min of running) to reach a steady state for easy/endurance runs. Therefore, the heart rate based method can not be applied with any training involving intervals or changing training zones. For example, 400m intervals can hardly be described in terms of heart rate as even at maximum possible pace the heart rate might only increase significantly during the third or fourth interval. Another example are runs involving changing training goals such as during Fartlek runs. The heart rate takes a certain time to adjust which is called the heart rate lag time. Heart rate is then a mere estimate of effort. Training zones can therefore not be applied as the only source of information and have little meaning to training above LT.

To circumvent this problem, I returned to an almost historic book by Jack Daniels (Daniels' Running Formula) which at the time had a great influence on many coaches. I personally find his ideas of training maximum oxygen intake (VO2max) unpractical (it was also discarded by more recent publications, e.g. by Steve Magness, Brad Hudson) as intense intervals at VO2max tend to put enormous stress on my body and provided little source of improvement in my case. Also, the concept of VO2max has little connection to running performance, LT is a much better predictor as it turns out. What Jack Daniels does provide though is an idea of the relationship between current pace at lactate threshold and all other paces. This is very helpful. Since we already know our training zones it is simple enough to make the connection.

The starting point are the tables of Jack Daniels where he started at the current (and recent) personal best time for a set distance (say 45min for a 10K). The tables can be found on the internet, even an Android App ("Pace+" by AvH) exists with similar results. Also, find a short summary for the paces concerned in this book in tables 47 and 48. If you plug in above example for a 10K personal best you will receive the following information:

	Pace +	Jack Daniels
Easy run	5:32min/km	5:31min/km
Threshold run	4:36min/km	4:38min/km
VO2max	4:09min/km	4:15min/km (interval)
Speed form	3:50min/km	4:00min/km (repetition)

Table 3. Advised paces for recent 10K race at 45min.

The information for Daniels tables I also found on the Internet in form of an Excel spreadsheet (http://www.electricblues.com/html/runpro.html) containing the information for various heart rates (e.g. for easy runs I used 136bpm for my own runs).

I will now adjust the method and thus we will use the table a little differently. My underlying assumption is that a race result does not necessarily imply a runner's current abilities as all columns of training influence the result. Thus, a given runner might be doing a threshold run too slowly or an easy run too fast. To circumvent this issue I changed the race time for a 10K until I found my current lactate threshold running pace to be correct (at around 163bpm). I used this pace because I had done a lot of threshold pace running prior but it also works with the LT test (LT HR corresponds to a certain LT pace). The method will probably work with all running paces which have been trained much in the recent past. If you only do easy or endurance runs you might as well match the easy run pace at your heart rate for easy running. Yet, I did not verify if this statement holds true.

For the sake of the argument, let us say that I run threshold runs (6K run with 163bpm avg HR) at an average pace of 4:20min/km. Now, the 10K race result (to plug into both the tables and the app) is

18

adjusted until the desired LT pace is given. The subsequent race time for the example used would then be around 42min/10K.

	Pace +	Jack Daniels
Easy run	5:11min/km	5:10min/km
LT run	**4:19min/km**	**4:20min/km**
VO2max	3:53min/km	3:58min/km (interval)
Speed form	3:36min/km	3:42min/km (repetition)

Table 4. Advised paces for recent LT run at 4:20min/km (HR 163bpm)

Table 4 shows the result of the two methods, namely the goal paces for the given LT run as well as the resulting race pace that should be possible in theory (42min here). The result now provides the runner with a much better insight into where he should be able to train were all his running abilities equally developed. Is e.g. the easy run at 136bpm slower than 5:10min/km a weakness exists. Based on this approach a runner has an indication which abilities to train and why he is not able to achieve the theoretical race performance. The difference between the two shown methods (Daniels's vs. pace+) also reveals that the goal paces do not exactly match for the faster paces. In the following, we will turn towards estimated race paces for certain distances much rather than using abstract (and not very helpful) concepts such as VO2max.

2.1.5 Pace based training for interval running

Following the method described in the previous section I use the running paces proposed by Jack Daniels to know the running paces for all runs where heart rate does not help. Especially for race preparation I use the method introduced by Brad Hudson who proposed that in preparation for any race especially the interval runs prior to the race become more race specific week by week. So, e.g. to prepare for a 5K race I would recommend intervals at 1.5K, then 3K and finally 5K race paces at the current training level (determined through current LT). These paces I obtain from the tables by Jack Daniels with the adaption proposed in the former section.

For the current example (4:20min/km LT pace) I arrive at 3:38min/km (mile), 3:52min/km (3K) and 4:02min/km (5K) race paces. Theoretically, a 10K time of around 42min should be equivalent to a threshold run at 4:20min/km pace (according to Daniels). If now one of the other paces is faster than a runner is currently capable this indicates that some ability is lacking. The columns of training would not be all on the same level. So if you run your easy runs really at around 5:20min/km instead of the 5:10min/km from Jack Daniels' tables training for basic endurance might be a path for improvement.

Since training is supposed to improve the running paces at a certain heart rate this method has to be repeated once changes in running pace become apparent. So either if a runner improves his pace (or even gets slower), the new running paces need to be recalculated and training will be resumed at the new level. It makes no sense to train at a level the is too high or too low. Let us assume that a training plan is geared towards improving easy and endurance paces it will in the future also be possible to improve the other running paces to this newly found level. The key is that the running paces for a certain level are always linked.

3. Developing the Columns

The basic concept of training is to introduce a stress which forces the body to adapt to said stress. If you run often your body will get used to running often. If you are subjecting your body to run at a high speed often your body will also adapt to that and be most likely able to run at a faster pace in the future and so forth. While this concept is easy to grasp for a lot of runners it is not easy to understand that the run itself does not make you better at all. It is the subsequent recovery period that leads to the recovery and supercompensation of the running abilities. Thus, two important concepts about training need to be understood:

1. Recovery needs to be implemented correctly into a training plan just as much as the training runs themselves and,
2. A workout needs to be merely hard enough to make the body adapt and improve the desired running abilities. Feeling completely worn out or subjecting yourself to a race situation in as many runs as possible is just not necessary and often times counterproductive. I once saw a documentary about a professional runner trying to make the Olympic team. He was proud to add two more intervals to a session of 10 times 1K on the track as he was sure it showed his dedication to his goal. I thought it could have even hurt his goal.

Following these basic concepts it is now necessary to introduce the different types of workouts and how they should be carried out to trigger the development of the desired abilities for faster running.

3.1 The column of endurance

The first and most important ability for any distance runner is running for extended periods of time. It seems rather trivial to say this but many runners still believe that faster pace, very taxing workouts are what makes you develop the ability to run at a faster pace. Although this can not completely be denied to be true it is still the wrong concept.

Generally, the body is limited in the endurance column by how much oxygen can be delivered to the muscle cells while not producing significant amounts of lactic acid. Heart stroke volume, the amount of hemoglobin in the blood and the capillary density in the muscle tissue are just a few aspects of what needs to be improved. The body is very slow to adapt these systems which is why it takes years of training to improve the endurance column to the maximum physical level of any given athlete.

Athletes of the time before jogging became a popular pastime often ran middle distance track races early in their lives. Races like 800m or the mile need a lot of speed development although even for these races the column of endurance is already very important. For anything beyond 3K races, endurance becomes the main ability to train for. This, and the fact that endurance takes a relatively long time to develop, places much emphasis on the development of this ability. This is even more emphasized for todays' runners. Most runners like myself begin their running careers with 5K or 10K races or even a marathon these days. Therefore, the endurance base, years of easier paced running, is just not developed much.

As a result, endurance training alone will most likely help improve a runners performance during the first couple of years of training. But how should you approach the subject?

3.1.1 The two basic philosophies of endurance running

Even though I introduced my view of endurance running through the definition of heart rate zones earlier this only represents one of two philosophies.

The first could be described as the long-and-slow approach. Runners do longer runs of 25km and more one day per week sometimes as slow as 10min/km (brisk walking pace). These very long runs (>3 hours sometimes) are supposed to train fat metabolism (which they will), prepare the joint-tendon system for long running and workout the respiratory system as well. While the concept has its place for runners attempting ultra distance events without having a sufficient fat metabolism I could not get anything out of those runs for any distance below the marathon. The subject of fat metabolism is key in very long runs. A runner has glycogen stores, which is a form of sugar the body can use as fuel, stored in the muscles and the liver. This fuel lasts for runs between 1.5 and 2 hours time (for pro runners on the higher end). Note that the body will react to depleted glycogen stores with reduced performance even though the stores might be still somewhat filled. The body plans ahead carefully and takes running pace, fitness and outside factors such as temperature automatically into account. Glycogen is a precious commodity the body likes to preserve at all cost as it is the only fuel source for the brain. Fat on the other hand is available almost infinitely (even in Olympic level runners being very light weight). If your body is now trained to burn fat instead of glycogen you will not see the negative effects of running for a long time. Also, of course, one can eat/drink a sugary substitute to help the body along. In summary, this means that most runners with 10K times below one hour will not experience a difference in performance regardless of their state of fat metabolism. I personally think that a race significantly longer than one hour (very conservatively) should trigger thoughts in the direction of fat metabolism and glycogen substitution. Thus for most runners, very slow and long running is not really what is most important.

From personal experience I remember at a time when I began to run competitively I was hardly able to get through 30km at a slow pace without glycogen substitution. My fat metabolism was virtually non existent. But only two years later all the easy running lead to very little need for glycogen substitution. I contribute that to easy running and also to regular long runs without breakfast in the morning which in my opinion forces the body to use fat as a fuel source. This lead to my belief in the competing train of thought that endurance will best be developed at the maximum pace still possible for sufficient recovery. This approach results in heart rate zones introduced in the preceding section. Easy runs and most importantly endurance runs will put stress on muscles, the joint-tendon system that is not too excessive but still triggers adaption. Also, the respiratory system is working sufficiently hard as well as the muscles. More importantly, easy running pace is still easy enough to help recover over-stressed runners while still maintaining (or even developing) the endurance column. As a result, all running paces are placed at the higher boundary of a certain training goal (e.g. heart pumping volume and others for easy runs). From my personal experience this second philosophy of endurance running leads to much greater adaption than the first one before (which I tried for around a couple of months). Also, I strongly believe, if a runner increases goal race distances over a long time (as many great runners did, starting with shorter track races and ending up with the marathon) he will show a highly developed fat metabolism as well as long as sugary drinks are regularly absent during long runs.

3.1.2 Easy and recovery running

In most training plans, the workout following a hard session is often times an easy run. I usually do an easy run of one hour @ easy HR. No warm up is needed for these runs as easy pace is warm up pace already. The goal is to make the body adapt to accumulated running stress. It will build stronger tendons over time, trigger the formation of more mitochondria and the run will also help with recovery.

Recovery will not be quicker compared between easy running and resting (comparing days of recovery) which might surprise. For some unknown reason runners even received a temporary improvement of recovery if a run (or even a race) is scheduled for the day following an easy day (compare "Recovery for Performance in Sport" by Inigo Mujika). For example, a weekend of an endurance run on Friday followed by an easy run on Saturday and a long run on Sunday is preferred over the same weekend with a rest day on Saturday as long as this plan will not result in overtraining altogether.

The difference between an easy and a recovery run is duration and possibly pace. A recovery run might only take up 20 - 45 min while easy runs take 1-1:15h. Also, when a new run is introduced on a day which was a rest day before start doing a recovery run first and increase duration to an easy run over time. On some occasions, if fatigue is really pronounced, reducing easy pace by up to 30sec/km is a good idea to prevent overtraining. But the very slow recovery jogs recommended in some books I find not suitable at all (e.g. 6 min/km jog for a 38min/10km runner).

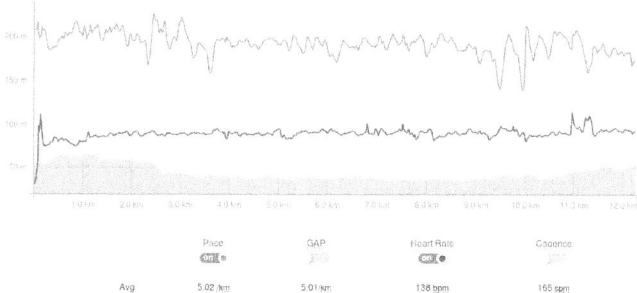

Fig 2: Example of an Easy Run: Heart Rate and Pace development.

Fig. 2 shows the development of a typical easy run. It begins at a slightly higher pace of about 15 sec/km faster than easy pace. After 10 - 15 min of running heart rate settles into easy HR and pace is subsequently adjusted to keep HR constant. Hills and wind will therefore result in a change in running pace. All in all, pace and HR should stay relatively constant as shown in fig. 2.

3.1.3 Endurance running

Endurance runs are great workouts to help make a training plan include more endurance running stress. Instead of doing all easy runs during a recovery week an endurance run helps improve the workout quality (more stress) without being too taxing. They are great to increase the training stress just a little without too much risk when you feel great during a training week.

Also, endurance runs can be used to replace e.g. a lactate threshold run if fatigue is all too great to carry it out. After warm up and legs feel heavy and the pace @ LT HR is much slower than expected slow down and switch over to an endurance run instead. Remember, sometimes less is more and who never adapts a training plan according to feel will most likely get injured on the way.

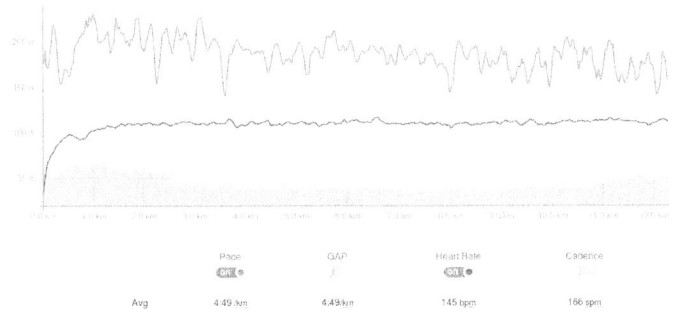

Fig 3: Example of an Endurance Run - Heart Rate and Pace

Fig. 3 shows the typical development of an endurance run. In every aspect it is carried out like an easy run except that the pace is higher. Since the first couple of kilometers are run a bit quicker than endurance pace it might well be possible that a pace right between endurance and LT pace is reached before slowing down to adjust for endurance HR.

From personal experience I found that the body seemingly develops the capacity to hold back on an oxygen deficit during the first 15min of some endurance runs. Say, endurance pace is 4:50min/km on a given day. I might be able to achieve 4:30min/km for the first 2-3km while feeling like easy pace. More importantly heart rate stays low during that time. Breathing and heart rate do not indicate the higher pace. Only after my heart rate has caught up (15min+) do I feel the pace and I will have to slow down to keep HR below the aerobic threshold in case of the endurance run. This only happens when I get used to the paces involved due to prior training. If I ran say a 4:15min/km pace (about LT in this example) my heart rate would jump above aerobic threshold before settling into LT HR. This experience is a hint that only very experienced runners can run purely by feel. Only after these first 15min is feel based running feasible. Also, I find this an indication of a good aerobic base. The body can deal with a mild oxygen deficit for up to 15min, something close to an aerobic buffering capacity. Such a buffer could e.g. prevent the body to skip into anaerobic metabolism during above LT interval sessions which is highly desirable as it provides a certain pace zone for anaerobic intervals. It might also show how an aerobic base is needed to make interval training above LT pace effective (which it is not without an established aerobic base).

3.1.4 Lactate Threshold Running

Lactate Threshold (LT) Running is another key workout for an endurance runner. While easy and endurance runs help improve basic endurance LT runs help push an important boundary. Above lactate threshold, lactic acid can no longer be sufficiently cleared in the blood stream which results in its accumulation. Through training close to LT, Over time LT will adapt towards faster paces. This is one important goal of training as LT pace is one of the best predictors of race performance over all distances. Also, LT runs help improve muscular endurance, the ability to run at a given race distance at a fast pace. LT runs are particularly important for 10K (and also 5K) races as this race is usually run close to the lactate threshold. But this type of run is also very taxing and takes up to one week of recovery time. The most taxing training weeks I recommend consist e.g. of an LT fartlek on Tuesday, an LT run of Friday and some LT at the end of a long run on Sunday. Such a week is often times directly followed by a (much needed) recovery week.

To carry out any LT run a runner should usually warm up for about 15 min @easy pace (may include a few short surges). After that he begins at his current LT pace (due to the tables by Jack Daniels) for his LT heart rate. The first two kilometers usually feel quite easy so any runner has to keep himself from running at too fast of a pace. Beyond that the pace will be adjusted to not exceed LT HR. Especially beyond the 5K mark a runner will usually have to do that. After 20 to 40 min the run is ended by slowing down to easy pace (HR will drop as much as to endurance HR mostly) and run for another 15 min to cool down. The cooldown should be treated as an important part of the workout as the body learns to metabolize lactic acid.

But how long should a runner run an LT run? We have learned that the concept of "the more the better" does not apply to endurance running. The duration, or more so if the latest LT run was too excessive, can be found out in a rather straight forward fashion. First of all, if you see your pace dropping significantly during the run end the workout. An example would be LT pace of 4:20min/km slowing below 4:30 min/km beyond 5 km. Call it a day and cool down! But often times the drop is more gradual and will only be detected after another couple of minutes at a slowing pace. Thus, it is advised to analyze LT runs on a regular basis in the following fashion after the run:

1. Write down the average pace and heart rate for every kilometer and place them in a spreadsheet.
2. Average pace and heart rate for the first and the second half of your run. The following spreadsheet results for an example 10K LT run:

KM	Segment [min:sec]	Average Paces	Heart Rate	Average HR
1	04:15		150	
2	04:17		158	
3	04:17	04:17	162	159
4	04:14		162	
5	04:21		163	
6	04:19		163	
7	04:20		163	
8	04:23	04:20	163	163,6
9	04:21		164	
10	04:19		165	

As you can see it is hard to keep the heart rate in check for the last two kilometers. Was this run too long for my abilities at the time?

3. Now divide the pace by heart rate, thus 4:17/159 = 0.00001869 and 4:20/163.6 = 0.00001842.

4. Finally, compute the difference between the two values in percent: (0.00001869 - 0.00001842) / 0.00001869 = -1.45%

   This value is nothing but the heart rate weighted pace average for the two halves of the run. The answer above means that my LT run was 1.45% faster in the second than during the first half of my run (since the paces themselves might give you a false first impression thus the weighted average). Note that values up to 5% slow down are still within the acceptable limits. 5% for the current example means if I had started with a 4:15 min/km pace for the first 5K I could have run 4:35 min/km for the second 5K and still be fine. I personally like to stay below a 10sec/km decline though.

So was the 10K LT run useful? The above analysis merely says that I was able to do the workout and really did do an LT run for the entire 10K distance. However, recovery is not taken into account. If e.g. this workout was done during a very taxing training cycle it probably put a burden on runs a few days later. A shorter LT run would be advised (also due to the fact that many coaches like Hudson and Magness advise LT runs up to 35 min at the most). In preparation for a half marathon race LT runs of e.g. one hour time at the end of a training cycle might be appropriate on the other hand. So it really depends on the situation and the runs later in a cycle.

Also, different forms of LT runs are advised to achieving different goals:

1. Sub-LT runs, although not strictly LT runs, are workouts somewhat slower than LT pace but faster than endurance runs. The reason why they belong in the LT run section is that they prepare a runner for longer LT runs. Also, sub-LT runs close the gap between endurance runs and LT runs. The latter aspect helps train all paces (and corresponding heart rates) that make out this gap. This is important because training makes running at a certain pace more efficient. If a runner never trains at a pace a dead space in his running abilities is

created. As a result, a useful progression for any runner is to ease into faster pace running, namely LT running, by starting with sub-LT pace over a comparatively long distance (e.g. 9km between 15min warmup and cool down) to establish muscular endurance and then increasing the pace week-by-week until LT pace is reached. If endurance HR is e.g. 144bpm and LT HR is 163bpm a sub-LT HR of somewhere in the middle of the two is practical with the corresponding pace. Start with the approximate pace for a sub-LT run and adjust pace to match HR after around 2-3km . Then, sub-LT HR is targeted for the rest of the run. The next week, a slightly higher HR can be targeted. This goes on until LT HR is reached several weeks after the progression was begun (e.g. 2bpm higher, which makes a runner reach LT HR in five weeks in our example). This way, a 9km sub-LT run can be stretched out into a 9km LT run. This progression is useful over e.g. a 4-8 week period. The downside is that the workouts require more recovery time due to time spend at high pace. Therefore, it is hard to combine the progression with e.g. a long run progression during the same period. This makes sub-LT to LT run progressions well suited for 10k race preparations.

2. The steady state LT run is often done on a regular basis (e.g. once per week). 15 min warm up, followed by 20-40 min of tempo running followed by a 15 min cool down.

3. LT intervals are used to extend an LT run that did not work out quite as planned (e.g. due to too much exhaustion induced by previous training sessions). E.g. after 20 min of running at LT HR the pace drops quickly by more than 10 sec/km. Then, jog slowly for 1-2 minutes and resume LT pace. You might be able to extend the LT run for another 5 min or more (see fig. 4). As with all LT runs and unlike easy or endurance runs, the starting pace needs to be known. Beyond kilometer four in fig. 4 the pace is adjusted to keep the heart rate at LT HR. At kilometer 5.5 the run became too taxing and a recovery jog (likely easy pace) is introduced before resuming the workout.

No walking should be done.

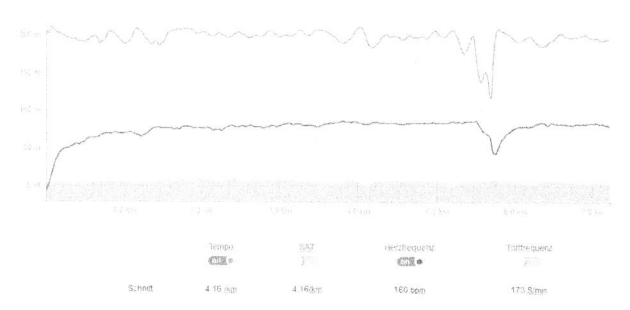

Fig 4: Exampe of LT run with interruption (warm up and cooldown not shown).

Another, and the most common, reason why LT intervals are used is when you wish to increase the duration of your LT run during a cycle. A runner might want to run a 20min LT run the first week, 25 min the second week and so forth. It is much better to split an LT run into 20 min + 5 min instead of ending the run at 20 min or even slowing down beyond. The total time run at LT is what counts. The week after that you might be able to achieve the 30 min as planned.

4. True LT intervals, as shown in fig. 5, are often used to help improve LT pace altogether.

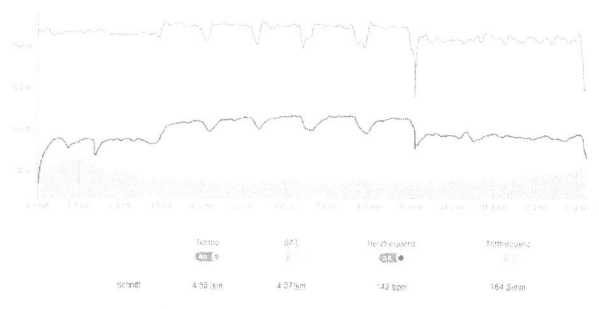

Fig 5: Example for LT intervals (5x1K@10K race pace with 1min recovery jog).

A strong endurance base allows for the improvement of LT

pace by running intervals (e.g. 5x1K@10K race pace) slightly above LT pace. The heart rate will not exceed LT HR, recovery jogs help metabolize lactic acid. Such intervals will not feel very taxing, but it is not advised to carry out too many of them. A total of 20-30min of fast work time is enough to provide sufficient stimulus. It is helpful to not let the recovery jog fall too far below endurance pace as the body metabolizes lactic acid better the closer the runner approaches LT pace. The hardest form of this workout is an alternation between 10K and LT pace (e.g. -5sec/km). This workout will provide a good stimulus to improve the ability to metabolize lactic acid with the downside of much recovery time needed. Thus, endurance or easy pace are mostly used as recovery to fit the workout into a training cycle.

5. LT Fartleks (fig. 6) are normally introduced into a training cycle when some LT running is desired but the status of fatigue is somewhat unclear.

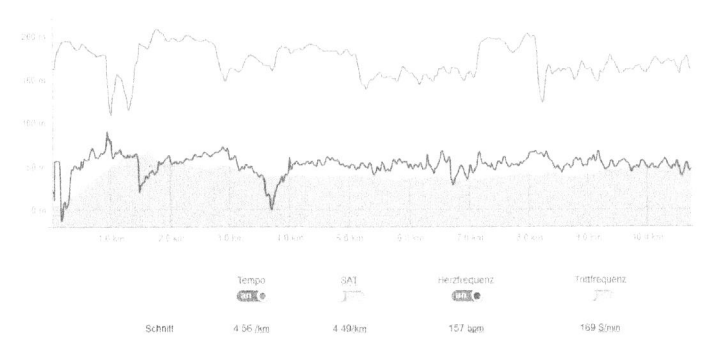

Fig 6: LT Fartlek (hill, different paces and recovery times)

Another reason to use them is to make sure the body does not get used to a monotonous training plan and to introduce different stimuli. Fartleks are great for this purpose. Generally, a runner has a number of minutes in mind (e.g. 20 min) that he wants to run at LT pace (the rest is run at easy pace as easy HR might not be reached). After warm up I usually run the first segment of the Fartlek with a specific purpose (e.g. a long steady hill LT run of about 3 min). In any case, I count the minutes at LT. After that I go by feel, sometimes a one minute section even exceeding LT pace (up to 5K pace, but not too much of that) with 3 min of recovery and sometimes 5 min segments at LT with 1 min recovery. The bottom line is that I play with LT type running segments and that the total running time should not exceed twice the LT time. So for 20 min of LT the easy pace segments for recovery should amount to 20 min as well (not counting warm up and cool down). This places a constraint on the amount of recovery I can do and it is also training my ability to focus as I have to count the minutes. I often times include hills into the LT Fartleks.

3.1.5 The long run

The long run is one of the important workouts for every runner. It is mostly carried out on a weekend day due to more time needed and often enjoyed in a group setting. In terms of pace it is more flexible than other runs as a wider range of possible adaptations exist. Depending on purpose, the long run makes up between 1.5 and 2.5 hours (for ultra distances it can be more). The shorter duration is mostly geared for short distance racing or to maintain endurance while other columns (especially speed) are more pronounced during a training cycle. The longer end of the run is suited for overall endurance development or leading towards marathon preparation with a few runs even longer than 2.5 hours (assuming here that marathon time is not too much below three hours). It is important to note that time spend at a certain stress is the important concept instead of distance at that stress. This is the real reason why faster runners accumulate so much more distance per week while their training hours might not necessarily be extended much. Considering this, I personally find a marathon race unsuited for novice runners who exceed the five hour mark. Starting out the running career with what is clearly an ultra running event for these runners seems too taxing for the body of a beginner.

Multiple long runs with varying training purposes result:
1. Basic long run (1.5-2.5h) @ easy HR (steady). Goal: basic endurance, develop steady pace over whole time, training joints, tendons.
2. Endurance run (1.5h-2.5h) @ endurance HR. Goal: more race specific for longer distance events, also a great endurance booster. Depending on speed, half marathon or 30K runs can be used as endurance runs. I like to do 2h endurance runs early in the morning with no prior food intake and just water during the run to train fat burning ability.

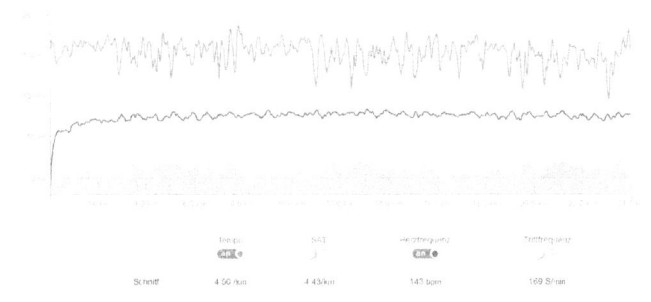

Fig 7: Example for a Long Run

Fig. 7 shows a typical example of an endurance long run. I begin with endurance pace and no prior warm up, after around 3km my heart rate reaches endurance HR. By adjusting my pace, especially on such a hilly course, I make sure that HR does not fluctuate too much and stays close to endurance HR. This can be quite a challenge, in the case of this run the pick up in pace at the end happened downhill and had the purpose of keeping HR up until the finish. Once a runner gets used to this type of workout, which is very taxing the first couple of times, it can be done very well inside a weekend half marathon or even longer races. Once practiced, endurance long runs make racing longer distances very enjoyable.

3. Long runs with pickup (1.5-2.5h) @ easy HR and LT (or sub-LT) HR. Easy running for e.g. 2h while picking up the pace to

run 10-20min of LT HR within the run. Goal: fat metabolism training, pace increases in races, LT development. This run is good fun with a training partner of similar ability. The last 5 min should be devoted to cool down @ easy pace (HR will most likely take time to decrease).

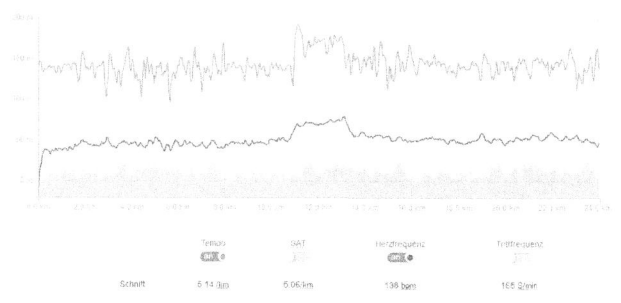

Fig 8: Example for long run @easy HR with LT HR pickup.

Fig. 8 shows a long run with a 2km pickup in the middle. Heart rate should drop down to easy HR after a few kilometers (around 3km in the example). This ability will improve after repeating this run a couple of times. It addresses the issue of race pick ups on the one hand, something a lot of runners have a hard time with. It also introduces a couple of minutes of LT running into a long run. Especially during an LT specific cycle this workout is very useful as different forms of LT running (e.g. LT intervals, LT stead run and LT run in a long run) can be carried out even in one training week.

4. Long increasing pace run (1.5h-2.5h) @ easy HR to LT HR). Start easy, finish hard. Goal: speed development in a long run setting. This is one example of many different forms possible in the sense of varying paces, maybe including some hills or trails. The increasing pace run makes sure that already fatigued muscles are getting used to the higher paces. The downside is elevated need for recovery time.

But why perform different long runs (especially of the kind mentioned in 4.)? The idea is to not do the same workout for run after run (as holds true for all runs) as the body will most likely adapt to the workout itself and not improve an ability. Many runners run the same run every Sunday which is often even done below easy HR. Doing even an easy long run every week might make it difficult for the runner to develop more advanced skills (e.g. to introduce a pickup in pace during a race). Therefore, the motto for all training plans would be to change the workouts around to never let the body get used to a specific one.

3.2 The column of power

The column of power refers to the ability of a runner to push his body weight off the ground to achieve a certain stride length. As running pace is basically stride length times leg turnover speed power is key to improving running pace. On top of that, a large number of runners (including myself) neglect the development of this ability especially during the early years of running competitively. Again it depends very much on previous training of a runner to evaluate the acute need for improvement. The lack of power can e.g. be assumed when a runner complains about not being able to keep up with the competition on a hilly race course. But the key is that a lot of runners are not able to improve their personal best times in road races due to the lack of this ability. The reason is that up to a certain point a novice runner can increase his leg turnover speed (higher cadence). But soon enough a maximum value is reached (usually around 180 steps per minute) depending on running technique (forefoot runners often achieve higher values for cadence). The stride length on the other hand can be improved much more (depending on the runners talent).

In my case, the neglect of power development was so severe regardless of training approach (speed drills, tempo runs, etc.) that my running pace would not improve. After I had introduced various types of hill running it only took a couple of weeks to see measurable results at all heart rates. The following types of workouts will help:

1. Hill Sprints: 15 min Warm up @ easy HR, then full out

(maximum speed) 8-10 sec hill sprints on a steep hill with around 2 min recovery of light jogging. This pattern is called alactic sprinting as no lactic acid is formed in the blood. The reason is that lactic acid diminishes the endurance column if introduced in large doses into the blood and is thus to be used for specific purposes only. The alactic sprinting workout is mainly designed to build basic speed on flat surfaces but can also develop basic power on a steep incline. A typical workout would be to begin with 4-6 repetitions and to increase the number of repetitions from week to week. It is important to not lean into the hill but to keep the upper body upright. No more reps should be done if running form starts to falter (upper body wiggles around or you start leaning into the hill). Hill sprints can be combined with easy or endurance running. Make sure the sprints are done at the beginning of the run after warm up to ensure good running form while you do them.

2. Stair runs. A popular workout among many coaches is the running up stairs e.g. in a stadium. A significant length in step should be used to increase the necessary power (steps in stadiums are often times twice as high as usual staircase steps). After the usual 15min of warm up lift your knees high and try to push down on the stairs with controlled power. I like the setup of alactic workouts (8-10sec with 2 min recovery) as longer workout phases diminish the endurance column but strengthen the ability to deal with lactic acid. The latter ability is important for race preparation but is not helpful during the phase of development of the basic abilities. A variation would be to run significantly more than 8 seconds but to watch that heart rate does not exceed LT HR. The pace will naturally be slower but the muscle exertion can also be achieved at slower paces.

3. Hill LT run on a steep hill @LT HR. After a 15min warm up use a hill circuit that is ideally the shape of a square (e.g. a housing block on a hill). Naturally, such a circuit has two steep inclines (one up, one down) and two horizontal parts

(one on top of the hill and one at the bottom). First, run up the incline at a pace somewhat slower than LT pace (for the first try it might be as much as 30sec/km slower) and try to run a steady pace up the hill while pace is adjusted to not exceed LT HR. On top of the hill try to jog (ideally at easy pace but I doubt that is possible at the beginning) the horizontal part on top of the hill and continue sliding into easy pace on the downhill and half through the bottom horizontal part. Increase your pace to the hill tempo pace you ran before while still running on the horizontal part of the circuit and then run the next uphill round. The number of loops should reflect current ability. Once running pace decreases significantly while it seems hard to keep HR below LT HR a runner should call it a day. The number of repetitions can be increased week by week. Fig. 9 shows an example workout with warm up and four hill LT runs and recovery on top of the hill and on the downhill. The pace is increased maybe by 15sec/km but since the hill is very steep LT HR is reached.

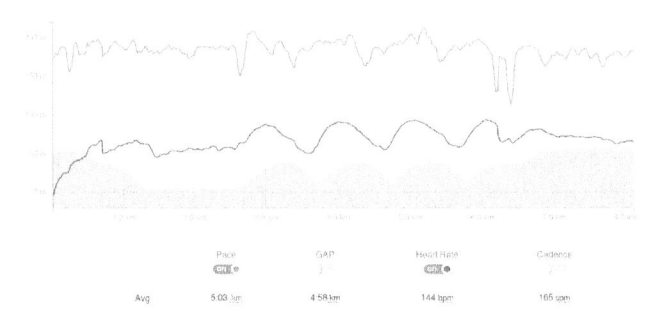

Fig 9: Hill LT run on a housing block circuit.

Ideally, the same pace is run from the first to the last loop (this is hard to do at first as the first loop is usually run too fast). What will probably increase as well is the pace you can do a LT HR up the hill over the weeks (from about 4:50min/km to about 4:30min/km after only 2 weeks and repeating the workout for the first time in the example above). For faster runners the uphill section can be increased in length but at first one to three minutes of uphill running should be sufficient. I found that this workout boosted my running ability very much if LT HR was not exceeded. I gained a lot of leg power but the fatigue in the following days should not be underestimated. Strictly speaking, LT hill runs increase lactic acid levels in the muscle significantly with the difference that the body will learn to transport lactic acid into the blood stream where enough oxygen in present (due to LT HR) to clear it again. Thus, transport and clearance of lactic acid is also trained as well as power without diminishing endurance.

4. Hill drills are a very useful addition to hill LT sessions I found in Keith Livingstone's "Healthy Intelligent Training". His suggestions go back to the methods introduced by legendary running coach Arthur Lydiard who applied hill tempo runs similar to hill LT runs mentioned above. In addition, hill drills were also used on every cycle. They were named springing and bounding. Springing is running uphill but instead of the normal combination of pushing the body forward as well as upwards the pushing upwards of the body weight mainly vertically is pronounced. The runner pushes his body off the ground and vertically into the air without moving much forward. This drill strengthens vertical force, more so since the drill is done on an incline. The opposite drill (bounding) works much like a triple jump movement. The runner tries to cover as much ground as possible while maintaining regular running form. The rear legs extends fully and pushes the runner far ahead. This type of drill helps develop the power to increase the stride length. Both drills can easily be implemented into a hill LT run circuit by e.g. alternating hill LT running with a combination of both drills. If a runner trains on a long incline (say more than 1000m) it is also possible to begin with springing on the first 100m or so, then run 800m LT hill run before finishing off with some bounding. But, a runner should be aware that the workout will probably not feel very heard yet the soreness during the

following days can be excruciating. When I tried them the first time I had to introduce a recovery week as I was not able to follow my training as planned.

5. Weight lifting. I am not a big fan of lifting weights in a gym for novice runners. This is mainly due to the fact that the column of power can still be pushed during power specific runs. Also, it is quite hard to do the individual workouts correctly. I did a lot of weight training in my early running days and did not like the effect very much. My legs seemed to increase in size and they did not seem to want to run at higher pace. This was probably due to doing too many reps with too little rest. Also in this case, alactic workouts (8-10sec workout with 2min recovery) seem the best case scenario. For professional runners weight training could be of importance as they have to push their bodies to the next level with extraordinary measures. In my opinion, this is not necessarily the case for intermediate runners.

6. Add-ons: Any form of power run mentioned above can also be added to an endurance or easy run as an add-on. Then, the number of repetitions or the duration of running is reduced significantly. Adding a little more stimulus or maintaining an ability are the two main aspects why power add-ons are used. An example run could be an easy run with a couple of hill surges inside the run or a staircase run after warming up followed by the rest of an endurance run. The key is not to do a whole power session but rather a small part of it.

7. Maintenance: Easy and endurance runs on a hilly terrain are vital to maintaining power beyond power specific training. Often times power improvement is a specific goal for pre-season training while other columns are in focus later. During these later training weeks the need to maintain power can be fulfilled by running easy and endurance runs on hilly terrain with short(!) surges in pace thrown in once in a while. The stimulus for power improvement is not very impressive yet for maintenance purposes it is just enough.

3.3 The column of speed

Another important ability is the column of speed to reach/maintain a high leg turnover or high cadence as well as running efficiency which is directly linked to the speed column. Also, the ability to endure higher paces for longer periods of time (e.g. during a race), a combination of endurance, power and speed which is called muscular endurance, is an important part of speed training.

3.3.1 Neuromuscular training

The first two aspects of the speed column has to do with a neurophysiological or neuromuscular training. Leg turn over speed or cadence is mostly subconscious in nature. The body defines a natural cadence which can be increased within certain limits. Also, what is often referred to as running efficiency is part of the training of the speed column and purely neuromuscular. As it seems, by training the speed column the body will also improve efficiency at slower paces.

The first aspect of the speed column is therefore cadence which is a basic ability. It is best trained through alactic sprints (8-10sec with 2min recovery). The reason for this is that below the 10-15 sec mark the body does not produce lactic acid as long as sufficient recovery is presented. Two minutes of recovery are often presented as sufficient in literature. Also, the workouts do generally not seem very taxing. I was very surprised how sore I was the following day after doing them for the first time. Alactic speed training can also be used as an add-on to easy and endurance runs.

Generally, alactic drill workouts can be done on hills to include training the power column (see the power column section) or on flat surfaces (ideally during an easy or endurance run after the first 15 minutes of warm up). Such a workout is also a great way to maintain the speed ability during long race, such as marathon race, preparation.

In general, any form of running at paces faster than 5K pace will help with improving cadence and efficiency. Yet, during pre-season, where mostly basic abilities are trained, high levels of blood lactate are not desired. Therefore, duration of speed training longer than 8-10sec are not helpful in this phase.

3.3.2 Lactate tolerance training

The second aspect of the speed column is much more present in many training plans. The goal is to improve the ability to run at fast paces for longer times. The abilities of leg speed and basic endurance as the foundation and the column of power are combined with (among other things) the ability of the body to

a) not produce enormous amounts of lactic acid in the first place,
b) the ability to use the produced lactic acid as a fuel (clearance of lactic acid in muscles and blood stream) and
c) the ability to endure lactic acid to withstand higher levels of pain (or maybe not really feel the pain any more?)

Especially the aspects of the accumulation of lactic acid are important the shorter and faster a race pace is compared to a runners abilities. It seems unclear today if lactic acid is directly related to fatigue but as every runner knows: runs at paces where high levels of lactic acid accumulate in muscles and/or blood stream are very painful.

To train lactic acid related aspects of running simply running beyond LT pace will theoretically do the trick. So I did a lot of 400m (@1.5K race pace) and 800m (@3K race pace) intervals with around 3min light jogging in between as introduced in a training plan I came across. I developed enormous speed over the course of several months but I did not improve easy, endurance or LT pace or my race results in the 5K or 10K. Thus, I found it was not practical to doing high paced intervals year round. Instead, following a period of base endurance development (see next sections) speed intervals have their rightful place and are even needed for optimal race performance in shorter races. For intermediate runners it can be discussed if speed intervals are needed for the preparation of marathon or even half marathon races if the runner is sufficiently slow. For example, I was able to improve my half marathon time from 1h55min to 1h45min over the course of 8 weeks by simply doing base endurance training. For 3K racing e.g. a similar improvement will not be possible in such a way, lactate tolerance speed training is needed. Some runners even showed that a great 5K race performance could be extended to a race as long as the marathon. A fast 5K personal best can be a strong starting point for an equally fast marathon even if that race distance was never attempted before (see performance development of German elite runner Arne Gabius who ran his first marathon below 2:10h).

So how is a race prepared assuming endurance and power are somewhat developed (let us ignore holding strength and running form for now)? Brad Hudson's and later Steve Magness' book introduced me to the concept of specificity. This concept implies that if you wish to train for a specific race, say a 5K, you need to train your speed ability converging towards race pace. Directly (say two weeks) before the race (5K in this example) you would do intervals (e.g. 4-5x1K with 1min recovery) @ 5K pace and a 20min tempo run @ 10K to 5K pace. Three weeks before it might be 4-6x800m intervals @ 3K race pace with 3min recovery and a 30min LT run that week. Four weeks before the race it could be 4x800m @ 3K pace + 4x400m @ 1.5K race pace each with 3min recovery and an LT tempo run that week and so forth. Like a funnel you approach the race pace from above (1.5K to 3K to 5K) and below (LT to 10K to maybe 5K pace). Generally, the next two slower and faster race paces are used to create that funnel. So for a 10K race this would be 3K and 5K pace from above and half marathon and marathon pace from below. The paces are derived from Daniels' tables as introduced in a previous sections.

Note that this concept does not work without a prior base endurance foundation. I used the concept unknowingly very enthusiastically without training my basic endurance first and it absolutely did not work for me. I developed an enormous ability to run intervals at various speeds including a final sprint exceeding 25km/h towards the finish line at the end of a disappointing 21min 5K race during my second year of running.

Generally, the total distance covered should be a little shorter than race distance. For a 5K race that would be 4x400m@1.5K pace+4x800m@3K pace (equals 4.8K); 6x800m@3K pace(4.8K); 4-5x1K@5K pace. For a 10K race it could be 6-8x800m@3K pace(4.8-6.4K), 6x1K@5K pace, 4x1600m@10K to 5K pace(6.4K) and 4x2000m@10K pace respectively. Though the slowest overall pace used is marathon pace. Therefore, marathon preparation uses a progression from faster towards marathon pace but not a degression from slower paces like with the shorter race distances.

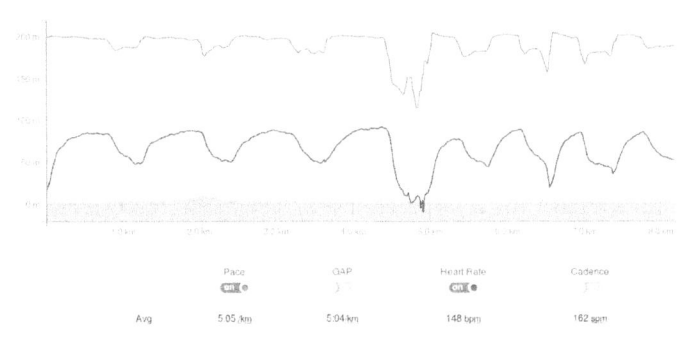

Fig 10: Example for 4x800m@3K race pace(400m recovery) + 4x400m@1.5K race pace(300m recovery) intervals.

Fig. 10 shows a typical combined 800m and 400m interval workout. Note that pace drops significantly between intervals but HR does not do so quite as much. Muscles on the other hand recover quite well. Since the pace of the intervals is higher recovery is also longer as more lactic acid needs to be dealt with. In my eyes, the length of the recovery phase shows what event a runner is preparing for. A workout such as the one shown prepares for a 5K run, as the total length of the intervals is closer to 5K (4.8K) and the recovery is long (around 3min). A 4x400m interval workout at 1.5K race pace with 1min recovery might e.g. be the final interval workout shortly before a 1.5K race.

The key concept is that most interval sessions will stress the muscles for higher speed with around 2-3min of active recovery making sure that the body learns to metabolize lactic acid better. The higher recovery pace (easy pace is sufficient) the better the body learns this, walking between intervals should be avoided. Another key concept is that the closer a runner approaches the goal race, the more race specific pace will progress which only works in combination with shorter recovery (1min) at easy pace. During all these interval sessions, basic speed as well as speed endurance (along with running efficiency and lactate metabolism) is trained for. Yet, a runner can only use these harsh sessions shortly (4-6 weeks) before a race as basic endurance is diminished by high blood lactate levels. This leads to the issue that improvements in speed will often be linked to race preparations for shorter races, the 5K is a very good example for this. Any runner will at some point reach a speed limitation which has to be moved out of the way by doing defined doses of speed work.

In addition to race specific progression, it is possible to introduce a speed block of a few weeks after extended base endurance training blocks to maintain or improve the speed column. As with all abilities it takes a lot less to maintain them in comparison to developing them beyond the point of current capacity. But doing speed intervals every week will most likely not get a novice runner anywhere. The training plans available on the Internet include them regardless every week because these training plans cover the last few weeks before a race only. It does not help using them again and again as a form of regular training as speed work substantially hurts basic endurance development.

3.4.3 The maximum number of intervals

Presented with a training plan that covers the final weeks before a race a runner finds interval runs to be included. The faster the pace and the shorter the distance of the race the more they will come in. Most runners know that the last interval should be run at the same pace as the first interval. This is generally good advice. But if a runner wishes to improve his ability of speed he has to venture into unknown territory. It becomes unclear which pace could be maintained even during the final interval. So how solve this problem?

As a first step, the method of finding the appropriate running paces will also help finding the appropriate interval pace. So if the plan prescribes 4-5x800m@3K race pace with 3min recovery you know what this should be for your current abilities (considering easy run, endurance and LT pace). Say this would be a 3K pace of around 3:50min/km for the example mentioned throughout this book. Now, after warming up for 15min as always, a runner begins the intervals. The first two should work out rather smoothly, number three is already taxing and the heart rate might increase above LT HR. It also feels like a jogging break should be done slower and longer than what is given in the training plan. During interval number four the runner might feel very exhausted: legs hurt, running form changes to the worse (e.g. cadence, upper body position, etc.). This usually begins beyond the 50% distance mark of the interval. Should the runner do the fifth interval or even more?

    A good rule of thumb in my eyes is that interval training should, contrary to common believe, not be completely exhausting (leave this for race day). A runner should believe he could be able to carry out one more interval at the end of the workout. The reason is that you wish to trigger internal adaptations of your body. During that fourth interval in the example the runner's body has already told him it is struggling. Adaption is therefore pretty much guaranteed to happen. Anything beyond this point will only put strain on workouts during the following days.

    Another reason to observe what happens much rather than simply following the plan is the fact that different runners need different intensities to trigger adaptations. Depending on a runner's (genetic and training) background and current abilities more or less speed work is needed. Thus, do your intervals until you observe the symptoms above (especially changes in running form). When in doubt, if the next interval is at a lower pace than the goal pace (e.g. 4:00min/km and struggling compared to 3:50min/km planned) do not even finish this one and start cool down. During the final stage of race preparation the race specific interval training (e.g. 5x1K@5K race pace with 1min recovery for a 5K race) is a great test of capability. This final speed workout should feel relatively easy, the last interval should leave room for more. If it does not, reduce goal pace of your race or prepare to suffer a lot. Especially important is that the recovery sections of these runs are run at least at easy pace to avoid surprises on race day.

3.4. The column of running form and holding strength

Holding strength implies the ability to maintain a specific movement pattern in the same way for a long time. A good example is that many runners tend to extend their upper body forward during the final portion of a race or during uphill running. Not enough strength (and of course muscular endurance) is available to keep the upper body upright. Apart from this obvious example many more instances of holding strength can be pointed out that are much less obvious but are the reason for many injuries. The reason is the ability of the body to adapt movement patterns. As a survival mechanism this ability is very useful as the human body is able to outrun danger. So if you force your body to run beyond its abilities the body assumes an acutely dangerous situation. It will then help to maintain the current pace even though it leads to wear and tear. The logic is to accept (relatively) small damage now to live and see another day (while possibly improving the skills tomorrow through supercompensation). For the modern day recreational runner this is not a very good approach. We exploit the process to finish marathons we might not necessarily be prepared for. Or even worse, we overuse specific parts of our body (joints are a likely candidate) on a regular basis and destroy those parts in the long term.

Running form, a related issue, has gained popularity as a training topic in recent years. Seminars, books, even on barefoot (so-called natural) running, instructional videos and other sources like to persuade the ambitious runner that changing his form ideally to forefoot running (at least to midfoot running) to avoid injury is needed. Recently, this argument has been called into question as a significant number of world class runners are found to be heel strikers. Also, mountain race (or sky) runners are likely to switch between fore-/midfoot running on uphill sections and heel striking on the downhill to distribute strain on the legs more evenly. Also, naturally occurring foot striking aspects like overpronation seem to play a role when judging running form.

Generally, the more a runner leans forward the more the foot strike migrates towards forefoot running. If someone wants to learn to run this way, leaning forward (which initially would feel very strange) is a great method to learn. Just try it during easy runs until your leg muscles hurt then switch back to you old ways. During the following weeks, slowly increase the distance of the new running form over time. I did this believing it would help my running pace (which it did not) and avoid injury (which it might have, no injury before or after). The bottom line is if you wish to adjust your running form it will take some time. Different muscle groups need to be developed for any new form.

What should be avoided in my eyes is the artificial adaption to a new form without thinking about what the reason to switch was in the first place. Forefoot running means to lean forward so your center of gravity is above or slightly in front of the point of contact between your foot and the ground. This leads to the energy being used to propel a runner forward rather than upwards. In reality I have seen far too many hobby runners (probably after taking a running seminar) who tip-toe around with their toes touching the ground (sometimes way) in front of their center of gravity. This scenario will likely do more harm than good to their pace development and it obviously looks funny as well.

Personally, I see many advantages to gradually changing form towards mid-/forefoot running (which really should be a gradual process). But these advantages, at least for myself, do not present themselves in terms of reduction of injury or higher running pace. Simply put, a more forward oriented ground striking position feels a lot more dynamic to me. Even though I am not actually running faster it feels like I am running more dynamically. This enhanced my pleasure in running. Also, when switching into a surge of pace or the finishing sprint during a race I do not have to adjust my form (nobody sprints all out on heel striking). Switching from heel striking to forefoot running improved some things but diminished others as well. Hence, I can not say that forefoot running is the cure for all problems. Today, I have no knee pain even after very long runs any more (which I sometimes did while still heel striking) but now I develop pain in my toes and forefeet which should not come as a huge surprise. This pain in turn can be dealt with by rotating my shoes (and regularly switching them out for new ones) and stretching my toes on off days. But still I enjoy forefoot running much more as it feels more fluid to me. But maybe this is due to my being a better runner these days? Who knows....

As a result, I call the almost religious transition towards forefoot striking form into question. It seems, like for so many other aspects of running (hello HIIT interval running), not to be the silver bullet it is often sold as.

3.4.1. Form adjustments as a warning sign

What seems more likely though is that any runner possesses a running form natural to himself. Or at least, the starting point is the form a running would use during the first section of an LT run. Of this running form a runner needs to be conscious, especially of the details. The following aspects are important:

- Position of upper body
- Position of foot strike in relation to center of gravity
- cadence

Especially during long runs and strenuous shorter races (e.g. all out 5Ks) the point when running form changes needs to be noticed. For any runner, this is the warning sign of your body that you have now surpassed the point of extended stress. This is not necessarily undesired. But a runner needs to be aware of it. If it happens during say the final 10% of race distance this is to be expected. But if it happens after 50% of race distance there is an issue. It can be many different things: you began with a pace that is too high for your current level of fitness and you now pay the price for it or you are not trained towards some aspects of the race course (e.g. hills, surges you did, etc.). If none of these aspects apply, changes in form are to be treated as the starting point of a search for answers. The following

might be the case:
- The holding muscles (upper body and/or legs) are not strong enough to maintain your most efficient running form over the entire race distance. You will get less efficient beyond a certain point, your pace will get slower (sometimes accompanied by increased cadence). For a forefoot runner this means you have most likely not regularly trained your holding muscles in the mid-section of your body (see holding strength column) and/or neglected the power column. For a heel striker, the holding muscles around the knees (and or hips) are most likely too weak (upper body plays a minor role here in my eyes) as well as the power column.
- It is important to have running form checked out regularly. This can be done during shoe shopping when a camera records your foot strike or while running with a friend who can run behind you and watch how form looks. Look for adjustment motions especially in the knees, ankles and hips. Say e.g. one knee forms a sudden jerking motion (often to the inside) during the moment of ground contact something is seriously wrong. Motions such as this and similar might wear out the affected joint, may lead to tendon inflammation and other injuries. The first action would be the introduction of strength training during recovery days. Keep in mind that even though e.g. the right knee is affected it could very well be a range of motion issues in the hip area. Therefore, range of motion and holding muscles are to be trained across the board. After a couple of weeks, the identified problem should have improved significantly. Otherwise, seek analysis by a professional as these issues will most likely lead to long term deterioration otherwise.
- During interval runs or speed drills faster than your current LT pace you might notice changes in running form. As introduced in the speed column section form changes tell a runner a lot about the current state of fitness. A connection between the neuromuscular system and the accumulation of lactic acid in muscles and blood exists and needs to be

understood. Alactic sprints on the one hand do not raise lactic acid levels. Regardless, after a certain number of alactic sprint intervals running form will change. Muscle fibers are exhausted, tears are present. This is the point not to continue with more intervals. On the other hand, lactic intervals will result in accumulation of lactic acid first in muscles then in the blood stream. This occurs even though muscles might still be quite capable and is the reason why you can force the final 500m of a 5K race through the pain. Your form will suffer regardless. Again, no additional interval is necessary to trigger adaption of lactate tolerance while muscle tear is avoided.

Therefore, watch out for decay of running form and end the interval running accordingly.

3.4.2 Training for running form

What happens when running form changes is that the body looks for ways to provide the required work output even when some muscle groups are exhausted or not sufficiently developed. Similar to the ability of speed, the form column is improved by improving power and speed while maintaining natural form. As a result, endurance at natural form will be the result. This will over time lead to race finishes at the runner's natural form (or close to it) as well. Watching race finishes of the running greats will reveal their sometimes seemingly superhuman ability to show extreme exhaustion on their faces while maintaining near perfect running form.

If subject to prolonged, repetitive work load, your brain automatically rotates to different movement patterns to avoid muscle overuse and therefore tears. A runner can force those changes from happening to some extent which of course will result in overuse and tears. A workout is just that, doing something the body is not used to so it adapts. It is just a matter of magnitude of stress and duration that sets the difference between a helpful adaption trigger versus a starting point for injury. For this reason, the long run is one appropriate workout to train form issues.

Forcing yourself to keep up the most efficient running form (natural to you) step by step for more and more time during a long run will train the ability of maintaining running form even for short races with higher paces. Let us assume for a moment that a runner has done hill LT runs and shorter easy and endurance runs in previous months regularly. As a result, these three paces have improved. Then, the runner attempts to extend long runs at the improved endurance pace (say two hours). He will notice that beyond a certain time of running (likely >125% of his longest endurance run to date, say after 1.5 hours) it will become increasingly difficult to maintain running form (it will also become more taxing, legs will hurt, etc.). This is because the runner adds a new stress to the body: running longer distance at the improved pace. A good training method is then to concentrate on every step of running and to force the natural form (of the first part of the run) as long as possible. This will be very challenging mentally and at some point a runner might have to give up and run with bad form. The holding strength of the body specific to the runner's form will be trained and the runner will most likely be able to maintain his form for longer in future runs. A downside of this method is that warning signals of the body are actively ignored which should not be done too often. Be aware that the next day should be a rest day and two days after a different ability should ideally be focused on which is not always possible. Restrictions (e.g. resulting from training goals) like this lead to accumulated stress: rest weeks will be needed depending on training load and condition of the individual runner. A runner should be aware of this effect. Ignoring it will lead to negative outcomes (exhaustion, burn out, injuries, etc.). I personally like the extended long run at good form as a method of training as I can do it during running opposed to in a gym. But I also happen to recover quite well from muscular stress. So I should say this is not for everyone.

Another way to improve form related muscles are alactic (hill or flat surface) sprints if a runner extends the number of sprints maintaining good form. Just as before, at least the last one interval will be a mind focus game. Regardless of running form, form specific strengthening methods such as form drills also improve running form (a lot). I just do not use them as I feel I can train for form in the ways described above. But my personal taste should not keep you from doing them. A lot of literature and form classes introduce form specific drills so I will not go into the details of the subject here. I feel like this topic is an example for the fact that different training methods will help different people to reach their desired goals as long as the basic training columns are improved. Just keep in mind that the claim "I did this drill for x amount of time and my 5K personal best improved" is most likely more feeling than fact. Closely related to the motion of running is the relationship the ability to hold body parts in place which is considered in the next section.

3.4.3 Stability exercises to improve form deterioration

One aspect of how to avoid long term wear and tear on the body is to focus on holding strength as part of training. It is in my opinion that this second aspect of the training column can not be fully addressed during a run. Stability training is what is on many runners training plan and it belongs there for every runner. But which exercises to do? Again, literature and seminars provide plenty. But how to find what is right for the individual?

The answer is not as complex as one might think it is. From the most basic perspective, every time a human being stands up or takes a step the brain controls millions of muscle fibers in a complex order and magnitude to make that specific movement possible. You might not have wondered so far why your head stays relatively static on your shoulders when you stand up or during a run. But when you think about it it takes tremendous (subconscious) coordination to carry out such a task. From a runners' perspective two kinds of situations are important:

- static holding strength to keep the location of a body part fixed in relation to its surroundings (e.g. your head on your shoulders or the upper body being kept fixed in an upright position) and
- dynamic holding strength to keep the relative position of a

body part during a repetitive motion in relation to its surrounding body parts constant (e.g. the knee should allow the lower leg to swing back and forth but should not allow a wobbling motion to the outside or inside, we would call that leg instability). This aspect is part running form (see previous section) and part holding strength.

It can now be safely assumed that the majority of holding muscles and therefore local holding strength is trained during every day life (e.g. holding the head upright) or during running (e.g. knee stability for me always was). Some problematic areas might not even have a detrimental effect on running performance or long term wear and tear. An example would be the upper body running form of Paula Radcliffe the current female marathon world record holder. Especially during the second half of her marathons Paula would bang her head back and forth. This motion is part of a less than stable upper body form which she has been criticized for. But this motion did not prevent her from becoming the best female marathon runner to date. Not only that but some biomechanics calculations suggest that the absolute best marathon time a human being is capable of might be as fast as 1h55min for men and around 2h15min for women. If this holds true, Paula's world record of 2h15min25sec (London marathon, 2003) might as well never be broken or if maybe by a couple of seconds. We can also safely assume that her upper body form has no significant influence on her (or anybody else's) race performance. It might have a long term effect which we might not know about yet.

The important part is that if a certain running form does not present an acute problem (pain, joint deterioration) there is little reason to change it. This approach leads to the following assessment procedure:

- Form deterioration: How is running form changing during interval training or at the end of long runs (e.g. upper body falls forward)?
- Form problems: Are there any instabilities in your form that always occur (e.g. knee wobbling inwards at every step)?

Any one of these issues has to be dealt with separately as different issues are underlying reason for what happens. Generally,I found the book "Ready to Run" by Kelly Starrett an excellent source of information as to which exercises address which issue. Form deterioration is the first and least problematic of the three mentioned above. Every runner experiences it during a tough race. It can even help you determine how well another runner is doing. In a major marathon race I once saw two runners on television who had beautiful form and identical (180 steps per minute) cadence. Their feet would hit the ground simultaneously for kilometers. While watching I realized at about kilometer 35 that one of the two skipped out of that rhythm, his cadence was now slower. I counted and found it was around 175 steps per minute. Right when I noticed his competitor did a slight surge in his pace for maybe 30 seconds. This left the runner a few meters behind, the gap increased slowly even after the surge in pace had ended. I thought the faster runner had noticed the change in cadence as well and used the slight weakness of his competition for his own advantage. The runner who had surged ahead ended up winning the race. An intermediate runner like myself might not be able to make use of a change like this as they are quite difficult to detect. Also, I would generally not compete for the win. But what it shows is that even world class runners experience the decay in form.

Once a steady state is reached in a person's level of fitness without additional stability training no such training is needed (by definition). Once measures are taken to improve fitness (e.g. hill LT runs) some but not all needed improvement will follow automatically in holding strength due to more running stress. A runner e.g. runs his easy runs at a faster pace and therefore trains the core body muscles a little more that way. But this training stress is usually not enough which is found during the last interval or during the later part of a long run. Improvement in one training column will automatically lead to a need for improvement in other training columns. This is especially true for the form and holding strength columns.

It is then important to focus on form during those runs as described in the speed column section. But this will present a training stress (followed by adaption) mostly for the dynamic holding strength muscles. It needs to be assessed which parts of your running form deteriorate and to come up with specific muscle training methods for that purpose.

Generally, a forefoot (also midfoot) runner will have the tendency to lean forward, wobble in the upper body and arms or even show instability in the neck (head starts to shake). The general exercises for these runners are core stability exercises (front, back and sides), neck stretching as well as basic arm strength exercises such as push-ups. I generally do these exercises (push ups) in the alactic form (8-10sec with 1-2min recovery).

A heel striking runner might also show upper body weakness (so the exercises for forefoot runners apply to all) but might also experience instability in the knees. Leg strength exercises need to be done.

As a result, a runner will have to come up with a number of exercises done ideally at least once per week (I do them on a rest day) to keep up and/or improve any weakness that hinders him from holding on to an efficient running form throughout a race.

3.4.4 Muscle exercises to overcome stability issues

The next step higher on the problem scale is instability that is simply part of a runner's form. I.e., their natural, most efficient running form is faulty in some area. This happens to more people than one might think. When I see runners in public I often focus on their running form and I observe e.g. that a runner's knee might make a distinct move to the side on every single step. On every step the knee has to compensate a force perpendicular to the natural motion of the joint. This might go on for years without any problems but will ultimately lead to irreversible damage to the knee. The worst part is that it does not hurt until it is too late.

How to find out? First of all, many runners go to a special running store to buy their running shoes (recommended). They have to step on a treadmill where a video is taken of their running, especially the moment of ground impact. A lot of times the video includes (or can include if you ask) the upper part of the legs as well. Look at the video and discuss what the sales person sees. Let them criticize your running form and let them point out problems. Do not discuss, just listen and think about it. This is the cheapest method as the sales personnel often knows more than the runner. The more expensive yet very accurate method is a form analysis. For this, your legs are marked for better locating position and a video of you while running on a treadmill is analyzed by experts. The result will be workout specific to your weaknesses. This is money well spent in my opinion, a one-time investment helping prevent misery for years to come.

After you found the exercises, include the general ones as introduced in the previous section and the ones specific to your form issues into your training plan and do them ideally on a weekly basis.

4. Periodization of training

Now that the possible training paces are introduced and the training runs are defined it needs to be understood that training has to follow certain patterns in order to optimize training stress versus recovery. This is especially important as different physiological systems need more time for recovery and/or improvement than others. While muscles need a couple of days in most cases tendons might take several month to adapt to training stress. Being unaware of this and especially how to react to this information I started with a weekly training cycle first. This cycle I would repeat over and over again.

4.1 The weekly training cycle

The starting point for myself to get into an organized training plan was a weekly cycle. It consisted of three so-called quality runs and two easy runs. When a runner starts out with three identical runs per week (which is often the case) the question is raised how to gradually upgrade the training to a more effective regimen without overdoing it and risking injury. Going from say three runs of 10km to five runs of 10km will most likely be too taxing. In many books a weekly increase by about 10% into unknown territory is advised.

I undertook the following steps into a training plan that I copied from a book. At each step I kept training until I found that I felt comfortable with the load. The entire cycle took me around half a year to get to the last step:

Step	Tue.	Wed.	Fri.	Sat.	Sun.
1	10K LT	-	10K LT	-	12K slow
2	10K LT	-	10K LT	-	14K slow
3	8K LT	5K slow	8K LT		14K slow
4	4x800m(3K) + 4x400m(1.5K) _3min jog	5K slow	8K LT		16K slow
5	4x800m(3K) + 4x400m(1.5K) _3min jog	5K slow	8K LT	5K slow	16K slow

Table 5. My personal steps with several weeks at each step

In the table above, LT refers to a lactate threshold run, slow was a pace somewhere below easy running pace and the intervals were done with 3min light jogging in between the repetitions. Over the course of one year I improved my 10K time by maybe one minute from 45min to 44min.

What I did right was a somewhat gradual increase of training volume over that time. I felt my muscles and tendons get stronger and got used to the overall volume. Also, I was able to pick up my pace into a sprint at almost every race I ran in at the very end. But I was not able to run at a faster pace during the first 90% of the race. I obviously paid no attention to my strength and weaknesses or different recovery times for the different physiological systems. From this training regime I can now draw the conclusion that I did work on the column of speed quite a bit more than I did on other abilities. The transition from training three times to five trainings started in a possibly good way. The volume was increased step by step over the course of several months. Slower runs were introduced while reducing the length of the lactate threshold runs at the same time. This led to a more balanced training plan. I admit this could have been planned in a much better way but it prevented injury. Thus, a positive aspect. Nevertheless, the slow runs were done at around 140bpm initially (pace around 6min/km) but with increasing fitness I watched the heart rate decrease to around 120bpm and I did not adjust my pace accordingly. This led to the slow runs to being not very effective. I was able to run for longer time and distance at those lower paces now which ultimately training muscles, tendons, etc. Especially for the physiological systems that need longer time to adapt to training this transition was positive. Also, I did the LT runs at 10K race pace effectively running a 10K race every week in the beginning. In addition to the intervals this training focused almost purely on speed, neglected endurance and power. I did do some weight training and worked on my form but did not see any effect on my running. So the ability to run races in a rather sluggish pace with an enormous ability for a finishing sprint can be directly related to this plan. In retrospect, I derived some good things and some predisposition for speed work from it which of course would influence what comes later.

What I also did right (since I copied that from an existing training plan) was that I spread the hard training sessions over the week and alternated with the slow ones. In literature these hard sessions are referred to as quality training sessions as they have a direct impact on certain abilities. I do not necessarily agree with this assessment as I feel that the lower paced runs are just as (if not more) important but for simplicity reasons I will use the notation. In addition to my setup of the training week there is another one making Tuesday through Thursday a training block instead if Friday through Sunday:

Tue.	Wed.	Thu.	Fri.	Sat.	Sun.
Q1	Easy	-	Q2	Easy	Q3
Q1	Easy	Q2	-	Easy	Q3

Table 6.Possible weekly setting for training runs

Q1 to Q3 refer to the quality runs (e.g. threshold, interval runs, etc.) where Q3 is usually a long run as Sunday is the most convenient day for most people.

To describe the transition from three days of similar training per week to a weekly training plan with some sense it is therefore advisable to start a change process in the following way:

1. Spread your three runs per week out according to the first week introduced in the table above.
2. Change one LT run (e.g. Q1) to an endurance run of one hour time (144bpm in the example)
3. Change one LT run (e.g. Q2) to the appropriate LT pace by switching to a heart rate based approach (163bpm in the example). Warm up 15min (easy run), LT run for 20-30min followed by a cool down for another 15min (easy run). Start at the lower end (20min) and increase to about 30min if you feel good about the run (I assume since the starting point was all LT runs, right?).
4. Change one LT run (e.g. Q3) to a long run at easy running pace using the heart rate based approach (136bpm in the example). Start also with one hour and increase the duration week after week until you reach 1.5 to 2 hours. You should only increase the duration of the run if you are able to keep a good running form for the entire duration (of that your form stays constant for the entire time if you have not concept of form yet).
5. Carry out each level of this plan until you feel like doing the specific run does not present much of a challenge. Then, increase the duration of Q2 and Q3 while keeping Q1 at one hour.
6. Once the maximum is reached introduce easy runs on the two days we left with no runs so far. Start doing easy runs (first for 20min) until you reach a duration of one hour for these easy runs.

The resulting plan should then look something like this:

Tue.	Wed.	Thu.	Fri.	Sat.	Sun.
Q1 Endurance (1h)	Easy (1h)	-	Q2 warmup LT cooldwn 1h	Easy 1h	Q3 long easy 1.5-2h

Table 7. Final Stage of a weekly training plan

If work or other aspects of life dictate it the alternative setup of a training week can be used:

Tue.	Wed.	Thu.	Fri.	Sat.	Sun.
Q1 Endurance (1h)	Easy (1h)	Q2 warmup LT cooldwn 1h	-	Easy 1h	Q3 long easy 1.5-2h

Table 8. Alternative setup of final stage of a weekly training plan

Obviously, the above training plan is not perfect and addresses some abilities (like speed) not at all. What are the advantages at this stage for a runner? First of all, far too many runners jump from a three day training regime into a five day per week plan and get injured. This is because the training volume (time) is increased too quickly. The described method takes you from around under 3 hours of training per week to 6 hours in our example (of course any time would do, just more time per week takes more adjusting of the body). It will probably take around six months to a year for the body to make the necessary adjustments. I always look for any of the following signs if the adjustment process went all to quickly:

- Resting heart rate increase of 10bpm above 4 week average
- Waking up in the middle of the night sweating
- Prolonged pain in joints or tendons. Especially knees, Achilles tendon (right where it attaches to the heel), feet (especially toes), ankles or hips.
- feeling of exhaustion and no motivation

If any or multiple of these symptoms occur it is advised to reduce training to three easy runs of 30min to one hour for the following seven days. Once the symptoms go away resume at the point before the last increase. If the symptoms remain after seven days (which never happened to me) you might want to rest completely until the symptoms are gone and possibly see a doctor. See the decrease in volume for a week as a good aspect of training as your body will not only repair but improve to meet the demands of the higher training load.

Depending on your natural talent, this plan, imperfect as it may be, will result in the following effects:

- You basic endurance should improve which makes longer easy running (especially with friends) much more enjoyable. Also, basic endurance takes a long time to develop, thus no time is lost.
- Many intermediate runners neglect their basic endurance capabilities and feel like only speed work means real training and improvement. Those runners will feel an instant boost through this endurance based training as they can still rely on the speed they build for at least a little while.
- The runner's body will get used to a variety of different heart rates from easy (e.g. 75% of maxHR), through endurance runs (e.g. 80% of maxHR) up to lactate threshold runs (e.g. 90% of maxHR).
- Six hours of weekly running is quite enough to achieve great training results while still not affecting social life too much. Of course more is always better in terms of performance but at this stage of going from three to five runs a week this should be fine (for some runners this means running more than 60km per week already).

But if this plan is applied for a couple of months the following negative effects will also be obvious:

- LT runs, while initially increasing in pace (remember we do them based on a max. HR) will level off and no further improvement can be reached. What is more disconcerting,

they feel like the runner had more than enough air to run an even faster pace but his leg muscles will hurt or simply not allow to go faster. I even had the situation where I could not reach the HR for LT runs any more. I just felt too tired in my legs. The reason is that you did not train the column of speed.
- If you attempt surges in a race or need them due to hilly terrain you will probably hate the experience. The reason is that you did not train the column of power unless some of your running was carried out on very hilly courses.
- The ability to sprint all-out at the end of a race will diminish after a couple of months. If you did speed work prior it would be very hard to do intensive intervals (more about those later) at the pace maybe once familiar. The reason is that you did not train the column of speed and especially lactate metabolism.
- Overall, longer races of more than 30min in time will feel easier than before as you seem to have "more air" while the speed for shorter races seems lost. The reason is that you did train the column of endurance a lot. This might feel unwanted to runners who essentially wish to run faster in races there is not way around building an endurance base first.
- Also, you might feel that at the end of a race (especially a faster paced one) your form changes for the worse. The reason is that you did not train the column of holding strength.

4.2 Monthly training cycles

To upgrade from a weekly training plan and avoid some of the downsides as well as the monotony of the final stage a progression over several weeks helps. I learned this concept first by following Brad Hudsons and Matt Fitzgeralds book ("Run faster"). They used the concept of specificity which was new to me and will be introduced in depth when we talk about race preparation. It mainly means that the closer you get to race day the faster the pace for your tempo runs (e.g. from LT pace towards race pace) while the pace for interval runs slow as the intervals get longer and recovery gets shorter (e.g. from mile pace towards race pace). In short, your runs get more and more race-specific. Race pace is approached like a funnel from above as faster paces get slower as well as from below as slower paces get faster. Specificity implies indirectly that a runner stresses out the body so much during a cycle that a rest week is absolutely needed to repair and improve. This was the main upgrade to the training concept I used before.

4.3 The base cycle

Taking the concept of the weekly cycle as the starting point using multiple weekly cycles to form a monthly cycle is the natural progression of the concept. From week to week, step-by-step a runner can progress towards a set goal for the given month. At the end of such a monthly cycle a rest week is scheduled during which the desired improvements take place. The problem here: different people can endure different lengths of training cycles of increased stress before needing a rest week.

This needs to be figured out for every runner before making year long plans. Therefore, I call them monthly cycles as mine lasts four weeks. But three weeks and more rarely five week long cycles are also possible. To find out about this personal need, I used a progressive plan with a standard four week cycle. The fourth week was a recovery week as the last week of a cycle always is. If I was too fatigued to carry out e.g. training week three I would replace it with the recovery week four instead and start the cycle from the beginning. I can mostly deal with four week cycles but sometimes I have to reduce to three. I always seem to show improvement during the recovery week and am able to start fresh and with faster paced running into the next cycle. This is generally an approach I recommend to any runner advancing. Forcing through the next given week does not help a runner improve, he simply wastes a week. Recover, start fresh(er) is key to getting better.

A typical 4-week training cycle could look something like this:

Week	Tue.	Wed.	Thu.	Fri.	Sat.	Sun.
1	Q1 warmup, 4 hill tempo runs (2min @ LT HR) with 2min recovery, cooldown	Easy + 2-4x 6-8sec sprints (1h)	-	Q2 warmup, LT (20min), cooldown	Easy (1h)	Q3 long easy (1.5-2h)
2	Q1 warmup, Fartlek with 20min LT HR with one hill and different paces, cooldown	Easy + 3-5x 6-8sec sprints (1h)	Q2 warmup LT (25min), cooldown	-	Easy (1h)	Q3 long endurance (1.5-2h)
3	Q1 warmup, 5 hill tempo runs (2min @ LT HR) with 2min recovery, cooldown (1h)	Easy + 4-6x 6-8sec sprints (1h)	-	Q2 warmup LT (30min) cooldown	Easy (1h)	Q3 long easy run with 10-20min LT at the end (1.5-2h)
4	Easy (1h)	Easy (1h)	-	Endurance (1h)	Easy (30 min)	long recovery (1.25-1.5h)

Table 9. Example for monthly progression in the base cycle

Above table shows a monthly progressive plan that could be the next step after the weekly plan has leveled off. It also introduces a couple of new training runs. These runs are designed to improve on some of the weaknesses of the weekly plan. Mondays are always rest days and are therefore not specified.

Tuesday e.g. is now converted to a day to improve power with hill tempo runs. These runs are carried out (after warming up with easy pace for 10-15min) at a steep hill that is long enough to run up on for about two minutes. The pace should start rather high with a maximum at LT heart rate. I use a course setup that looks almost like a square with a steep hill, a flat top where I can catch my breath with

66

a slow jog, going down the hill on the other side still rather slowly before picking up the pace close to the bottom of the hill to go for another round. The pace depends on the incline and on the level of fitness of course but LT heart rate should not be exceeded. The second week is a Fartlek run on a hilly course where (again after warmup) I like to run one long hill up and then farther on a flat surface or even slightly downhill at times. I only count the minutes I have run at fast pace limited by LT heart rate. Sometimes that means a few 1 min high tempo intervals, sometimes it means 5 min LT type parts. Combine as you feel and try to get a little bit of everything into it. The third week is basically an endurance run with a couple of 8 sec sprints (all you have to offer) after warm up with 2 min of easy running as recovery. This should help with speed, the hill running sections with power. The progression seems to get easier every week but I found that I fatigue more and more every week leaving the first training week with the hardest workout.

Sundays are now used to practice different types of long running. From the already familiar easy long run in the first week over the increased pace endurance long run to an easy long run with some tempo running at the end. Note that especially the long run leads to adaption of the body to the form of training itself. I.e., if you always do the same easy long run on Sundays, a longer race (e.g. 15K or half marathon) will feel most unfamiliar. You must change the long run every week. The described progression introduces enough stress to increase the long running ability to a point where the runs are very enjoyable yet still challenging.

Doing this progressive monthly program for the first time might result in a lot of runs that can not be carried out fully. But it should be possible to increase the number of hill repetitions or the duration of the endurance part of the long run or the LT part during the next cycle until the described cycle is fully carried out.

It is important to note at this point that a plan like this, which could be much too ambitious for many runners, is a guideline to improve along. Do not follow this or any plan religiously as they are not designed for you. Do as much as needed to carry out a taxing yet not totally exhausting workout. It is better to be able to recover for the next run than to maybe cut a training cycle short because of a single workout done too intensely. At the end of each run a runner should be able to say: "I could have done one more interval", or "10 more minutes", etc. The idea is to improve with the least amount of work not the most.

This monthly cycle does now present some additional advantages over the weekly cycle:

- For enhancing muscle, heart and respiratory capabilities, the weekly plan is appropriate. To increase power and muscle growth as well as the improvement of endurance the monthly cycle is much better suited as a runner can train above his personal limit and then step away from said limit by employing the recovery week.
- Power and speed will at least be maintained but probably be enhanced.
- LT runs can be increased in length taking into account that a new cycle might have let to a faster LT pace.

The downside of this monthly progression is on the other hand:

- Prolonged speed training above the LT threshold which is needed for race specific preparation has no room in this cycle.
- LT runs might still fall short in speed as the muscles are fatigued from hill running and can not easily show LT improvements.
- After a couple of months the runner's body has again adjusted to the training itself meaning that the cycle lacks the stress needed for further advancement.

Overall, the fitness of the runner should improve with this cycle especially if it is applied two to three times in a row. Naturally, different monthly cycles are possible. The one presented above is an example for a cycle emphasizing the basic abilities of endurance, power and speed without the finishing touches towards speed endurance or even race preparation. Therefore, such a cycle can be called a base cycle.

The base cycle (one that is suited for your needs at least) is very useful especially for the intermediate runner. The reason for this is that a runner will improve his easy and endurance running paces with such a training cycle. This will set the foundation (the base) for the improvement of LT running pace and ultimately also faster paces in later training cycles. The intermediate runner will climb to new levels of fitness towards his personal maximum. This is different for a pro runner as they have already achieved a level of fitness close or even at their personal maximum. Their training will also have a base phase but with less dramatic effects.

It is useful to run easy and endurance runs on the same course at least once a month to compare fitness levels.

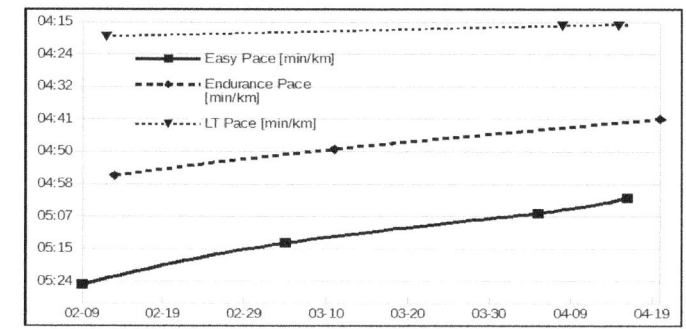

Fig 11: Development of Easy, Endurance and LT paces through base cycles.

In Fig. 11 the average pace during standard runs are shown for my first using the base cycle (three times in a row). My easy and endurance paces improved significantly. Easy running pace improved by around 23sec/km, endurance pace by 15sec/km and LT pace by 3 sec/km over the course of less than three months. Such an improvement is rather unlikely for a seasoned runner but one might comment that if skills are vastly lacking (such as my own were) they develop quickly. Significant is that easy running pace improved more than endurance pace while LT pace almost stayed constant. This is typical for the base cycle and shows its limits rather well. It also showed that my endurance column was vastly underdeveloped in comparison to muscular endurance and speed.

If a runner trains according to the base cycle month after month he will experience that easy and endurance pace will improve but LT will not that much. The gap between the paces will reduce. In the example above, the difference between easy and LT pace reduced from 1min6sec per km down to 46sec per km after the third cycle. Additionally, I felt "flat" especially during the LT runs later in the cycle. Keep in mind I often did not feel like doing alactic sprints which I paid for. During the LT runs I had thus the feeling that I was limited by the speed of my legs. My heart rate stayed relatively low but my legs started to hurt very soon as if I was dragging some weight along with me. I seemed to have been limited by some factor, my power and base endurance where there but I was not able to translate this into a faster pace at LT HR. So I seemed to be limited by another column that was underdeveloped relative to the improvement I had accomplished. The speed column seemed neglected.

Adding more speed focused workouts into the base cycle might reduce some of that issue. The resulting base cycle could look something like shown in table 10. Three aspects have been altered: 1.) the Fartlek has been replaced with alactic and 30sec sprints adding speed work and possibly a little loss of endurance along with it, 2.) an additional and even increased hill LT running was added, 3.) instead of increasing the length of LT runs a standard length (e.g. 40min) is carried out quicker and quicker adding to muscular endurance while covering multiple training loads. This approach should take care of the neglected speed column although it can only work so far. Eventually, different stimuli need to be introduced.

Week	Tue.	Wed.	Thu.	Fri.	Sat.	Sun.
1	Q1 warmup, 4 hill tempo runs (2min @ LT HR) with 2min recovery, cooldown (0:45h)	Easy + 2-4x 6-8sec sprints (1h)	-	Q2 warmup, sub-LT (90% LT) (40min), cooldown	Easy (1h)	Q3 long easy (1.5-2h)
2	Q1 warmup, 4x30sec sprints + 4-6x8sec sprints with 2min recov., cooldown	Easy + 3-5x 6-8sec sprints (1h)	Q2 warmup sub-LT (95% LT) (40min), cooldown	-	Easy (1h)	Q3 long endurance (1.5-2h)
3	Q1 warmup, 6 hill tempo runs (2min @ LT HR) with 2min recovery, cooldown (1h)	Easy + 4-6x 6-8sec sprints (1h)	-	Q2 warmup LT (40min), cooldown	Easy (1h)	Q3 long easy run with 10-20min LT at the end (1.5-2h)
4	Easy (1h)	Easy (1h)	-	Endurance (1h)	Easy (30 min)	long recovery (1.25-1.5h)

Table 10: Base cycle with more focus on speed.

In the example (fig.11), it is also roughly visible that the improvement even for easy pace slows down over time, the cycle becomes less effective (even with changes introduced as in table 10). This is typical for all training cycles. Repeated multiple times, the body gets used to the combination of different stresses and workouts. So even if complex monthly cycles are employed a fundamental change in strategy is needed after some time. For intermediate runners, who often lack basic endurance, the base cycle (one that is designed for you) should be repeated until the mentioned slower improvement and flatness at higher paces is observed. Then, the next step needs to be taken, the building of LT related speed.

For experienced athletes who have build their basic endurance it is also possible to employ a base cycle that I would call the advanced base cycle at this point. The goal is to improve the columns of speed and power as much as possible while also improving LT pace. Note, that the risk of injury for this plan is rather high so care which renders this cycle as a theoretical option only for most. Yet, for runners with the ability to sustain lots of fast pace running and general injury resistance the following base cycle is a viable option.

Week	Tue.	Wed.	Thu.	Fri.	Sat.	Sun.
1 (Monday: always stability traiing and an optional slow bike ride of up to 1h)	Q1 6x1min@3K 4min Recovery + 10x30sek@1.5K 2min Recovery (1h)	Q2 Bike 10x2min high resistance @60rpm 2min Recovery (1h)	Easy run (1h)	Q3 5K@LT + 2x800m @10K (1h)	Easy bike ride (1h)	Q4 long easy (1.5-2h)
2	Q1 8x1min@3K 4min Recovery + 10x30sek@1.5K 2min Recovery (1h)	Q2 Bike 10x2min high resistance @60rpm 2min Recovery (1h)	Recovery run (1h)	Q3 8x1K@10K 2min Recovery (1h)	Endurance run (1h)	Q4 long easy (1.5-2h)
3	Q1 3x400m@5K 4min Recovery +4x1min@3K 4min Recovery + 10x30sek@1.5K 2min Recovery (1h)	Q2 Bike 10x2min high resistance @60rpm 2min Recovery (1h)	Easy bike ride or recovery run (1h)	Q3 6K@LT + 2x800m @10K (1h)	Easy bike ride or recovery run (1h)	Q4 long easy (1.5-2h)
4	Fartlek (1h)	Easy bike ride (1h)	Easy run (1h)	-	Recovery (30 min)	long recovery (1.25-1.5h)

Table 11: Advanced base cycle with focus on speed and power.

Table 11 shows the advanced base cycle. The foundation is consistent running of around six hours per week while this plan contains up to eight hours of training. The difference is that only four to five sessions per week are actually running exercises while the rest employs bike riding as an alternative. As will be noted in the discussion about cross training below cycling does not present the runner with the same amount of joint and tendon strain while being very effective to train the power column. As a result, it is possible to

73

train for speed and running economy on Tuesday while putting a heavy emphasis on the power column every Wednesday. Fridays are reserved for LT pace training and Sundays will be the long run. Overall the cycle uses four instead of the usual three Q sessions. Ideally, muscle fatigue will be very high and the runner will advance quite significantly in only a short period of time. The downside is the relatively high risk of injury during this cycle. Q1 sessions put a lot of strain on tendons which can lead to inflammation. For many runners, half the number of prescribed intervals is more than enough to reach improvement. This, a runner has to find out through trial and error. In my experience, either right during the interval session acute problems will be knows or a couple of days later through inflammation reactions. In both cases, recovery should be used, ending the interval session in the former and a recover jog instead of a Q session in the later situation. In any case, injury will render weeks if not months of training obsolete. Thus, a week of easy running to avoid injury is always the better bargain.

In detail (table 11), Q1 thus begins with 1.5K and 3K running in a 1-to-4 scheme meaning that 1 minute of interval running is complimented by 4 minutes of recovery jogging (ideally close to easy pace). This is done because the faster paces introduce a lot of lactate in the muscles which is not flushed out into the blood stream (due to the duration of the work interval). During the recovery period with excess oxygen (easy pace) the lactate is again turned into fuel and the lactate level never rises significantly. This can be observed through the heart rate staying relatively low (much below LT HR).

Wednesday then covers the power column. Ideally, a spinning bike is used with work intervals set to high resistance and recovery intervals at a resistance which would normally lead to easy HR. It is important to choose a resistance that can be endured through the entire session. It is important not to exceed the low cadence of 60 rpm during the power intervals and to increase cadence to above 90 during recovery. If no spinning or stationary bike is available a long steep hill should be used which is repeated ten times in a low gear. For both possible setups the session should be done in a sitting position. During week two and three resistance should be increased slightly to get the body used to higher resistance.

Friday, however, presents an alternative setup of LT training which can also be used for the regular base cycles. One week of steady LT running is alternated with a week of LT intervals. Of course steady LT runs are going to be slightly slower and shorter than LT intervals and the sessions train different abilities. Steady LT runs bring all columns of training together: lactate is produced in the muscles and has to be cleared continuously, muscles and basic endurance as well as speed and running economy are only few aspects needed. LT intervals however present the body with two different problems: a slightly higher pace needs to be run which is accompanied by higher lactate production. Yet, the recovery intervals introduce the problem of lactate clearing on quite a high level. The intervals can roughly be run around 10K pace which will prove challenging. On top of this, the 5K (6K) steady LT run will be prolonged by up to two 800m intervals at around 10K pace which may or may not be doable.

Sunday, Q4, is of lower priority. In many cases, muscles will hurt to an extent which makes two hours of running almost impossible. Make sure to perform at least 1.5 hours of easy running to maintain basic endurance. Faster pace running is not needed nor dos it seem possible for Q4. I sometimes try to run endurance pace during week three Q4 which I am able to endure for 15km. After that I am mostly too fatigued, running pace drops to about easy pace while heart rate stays high.

Through weeks one to three more and more easy or endurance are replaced with easy bike rides to limit tendon fatigue.

The results of the advanced base cycle, however, are excellent. Throughout all heart rate zones, paces should improve quite significantly. Fig. 12 shows the development of easy, endurance and LT paces through one of my own base cycles. The shown data represent the advanced base cycle which was preceded by another advanced base cycle which showed excellent improvement as well. In only a couple of weeks it was possible to advance LT pace from about 4:11min/km to around 4:06min/km. This is no surprise as speed and power should have been improved. But, even though the paces were hardly trained for, easy and especially also endurance pace were observed to be significantly faster. Easy pace improved from around 5:00min/km to around 4:55min/km and endurance pace from 4:50min/km to around 4:40min/km.

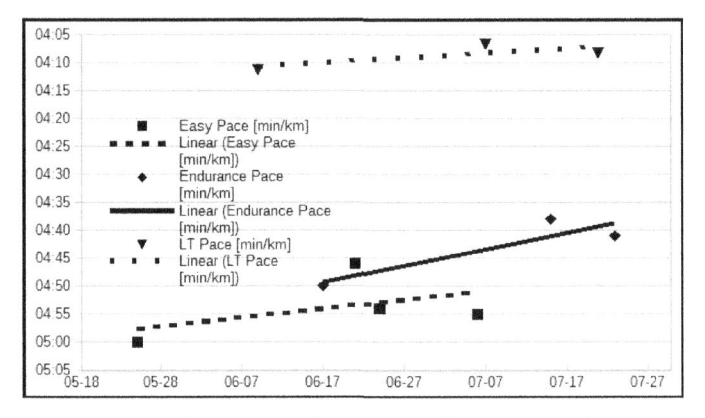

Fig 12: Development of Easy, Endurance and LT paces through advanced base cycle.

It is obvious that this improvement, especially for the slower paces, is overshadowed by muscular fatigue. The tapered improvement might thus even be greater. However, one aspect proves important especially for the case of significant improvement: while 10K to marathon paces will have improved as well a following build and prep/race cycle has to extend the newly developed physical abilities to actually get used to running a certain distance at the newfound pace. The rule always applies: develop the columns of running first and then get used to running extended distances at race pace. Therefore, training in one to several base cycles is merely the first step for improved performance.

4.4 The build cycle

One of the most effective predictors of race performance (especially 10K and 5K) is LT pace. It must therefore be our goal to emphasize its improvement. The foundation for this endeavor is always the base phase. If a runner tries to skip it, as many runners do, trying to advance LT pace will result in passing LT and really doing lactate heavy runs instead. E.g. your current LT pace might be around 4:15min/km and you try tempo runs at 4:05-4:10min/km as a training stimulus. The body will rely heavily on the lactic acid path of the internal fuel system. You will temporarily get faster but at a heart rate most likely above LT HR. This evolution is hardly productive as LT pace will get stuck. If easy run and endurance pace on the other hand improve through the base cycle, LT pace is underdeveloped relative to those paces. Under these circumstances a similar workout will most likely lead to an improved LT pace. The body, instead of mobilizing through the lactate path, will rely on the aerobic path which essentially means that oxygen can be supplied to the muscles in larger amounts than necessary for this pace at or slightly above LT. Thus, LT pace will advance to higher paces. Of course, it is more complicated than just this one workout. But the tendency is that a different foundation results in different outcome for the same workout in the following cycle: the cycles are linked!

So how to make use of the enhanced basic endurance capabilities? We have emphasized endurance, power and basic speed during the base phase (in the example three base cycles). Now, more race specific speed, LT HR running in different ways and maintenance of the basic abilities will be important. The goal is to overcome the downsides of the base phase while not reversing its effect. This presents a difficult task. If a runner steps to heavily on the gas and employs lactic intervals (e.g. weekly 400m Intervals @3K race pace) the endurance column will suffer. Easy and endurance pace will decrease which is a good way to measure the effect. Therefore, a cycle needs to be defined that links race specific preparation and base phase: the build phase (named after Joe Friels "Total heart rate training"). Friel introduces the different phases for the sport of triathlon where the columns of training need to be in precise alignment as the training load is normally much higher than for the individual sports while base endurance is more emphasized for intermediate triathletes in comparison to runners. Friel also introduces more than just three phases but for the start three should be sufficient for our purpose.

Week	Tue.	Wed.	Thu.	Fri.	Sat.	Sun.
1	Q1 warmup, 5x1K@LT pace 1min recovery, cooldown	Endurance 6 Hill Sprints (1h)	-	Q2 warmup, LT (25min), cooldown	Endurance (1h)	Q3 long easy run with 10-20min LT at the end (2h)
2	Q1 warmup, 6x1K@10K race pace 1-2min recovery, cooldown	Endurance 2 Times Hill Circuit (1h)	-	Q2 warmup LT (30min), cooldown	Easy (1h)	Q3 long endurance (2h)
3	Q1 warmup, Fartlek with 10min LT HR + 10 min above LT with one hill and different paces, cooldown	Endurance (1h)	-	Q2 warmup LT (30-35min) cooldown	Endurance (1h)	Q3 long easy run with 10-20min LT at the end (2h)
4	Easy (45min)	-	Easy 1x90sec Intervall @10K pace (1h)	Test Race e.g. 10K	Recovery (slow) (45min-1h)	long Easy possibly slower (1,5h)

Table 12: Example for Build cycle

A typical build cycle of once again one month duration is presented in Tab. 12. The cycle now contains up to three LT type runs per week to help close the gap between base running and the needed lactate heavy intervals for speed development that come in later cycles. Tempo intervals slightly faster than LT pace (10K pace here) will help improve LT pace if other LT running is present (here LT HR run as well as LT at the end of a long run). For this to work a good endurance base is necessary. The fartlek in week 3 is supposed to introduce some passages of higher tempo (around 5K pace here) but can also be replaced with 7x1K@10K race pace depending on how fatigued a runner is. The reason for the fartlek run is that it is unclear in advance how much fatigue will be experienced by the runner. Fartleks present the opportunity to run anything between an endurance run with some tempo and longer tempo runs with hills. The idea is to not go overboard and slide into an injury as this cycle is very tempo heavy. I suspect most runners will find themselves not being able to introduce a lot of tempo running in week 3. This cycle increases duration and maybe pace in Q1 and duration in Q2 while LT pace could increase as well depending on level of fatigue. Easy and endurance pace should stay almost the same or even decrease in pace a little. All in all, this cycle is very demanding while also putting heavy emphasis on LT-specific speed development.

The build cycle also needs more adjustment depending on the runner. It is entirely possible that Q1 has a lower number of intervals (maybe 3 to 4 from week 1 to 2) or that Q2 turns out shorter because LT pace decreases too much. The bottom line is that the body is subjected to the needed stress to improve LT (and maybe some faster) pace. For some people the needed stimulus is smaller, for some (mostly faster) runners a higher stimulus is needed. Therefore, keep in mind that a certain level of fatigue should be reached at the end of a defined run and that over the four weeks the fatigue will accumulate. If you stress your body out too much though you might have to cut the cycle short and switch to a recovery week prematurely rendering the training cycle less effective. This is especially true for LT runs on Friday. During the recovery week the muscles should hurt quite a bit on Tuesday and maybe even still on Thursday, you might feel quite flat and unwilling/unable to pick up the pace. So stay with easy running and possibly even a slower pace on Thursday if needed. The one interval at race pace is run to prepare the muscles for the faster running on Friday. Even though this would not be an ideal race preparation (we will come to that later) test races are important to see how far you have improved.

Also, during the build phase, a Sunday long run is sometimes replaced with a minor race with the difference that a 10K race is then run at LT HR and the LT run on Friday is replaced with an endurance run (see table 13). The day before such a race (Saturday in this case) would be an easy day with again one interval at race pace. The recovery week, as it directly follows the race weekend will be taken

79

more lightly and the test race is omitted. It is also possible to try running the race at a pace faster than LT pace but I doubt you would be rested enough to attempt that.

Week	Tue.	Wed.	Thu.	Fri.	Sat.	Sun.
1	Q1 warmup, 5x1K@LT pace 1min recovery, cooldown	Endurance 6 Hill Sprints (1h)	-	Q2 warmup, LT (25min), cooldown	Endurance (1h)	Q3 long easy run with 10-20min LT at the end (2h)
2	Q1 warmup, 6x1K@10K race pace 1-2min recovery, cooldown	Endurance 2 Times Hill Circuit (1h)	-	Q2 warmup LT (30min), cooldown	Easy (1h)	Q3 long endurance (2h)
3	Q1 warmup, Fartlek with 10min LT HR + 10 min above LT with one hill and different paces, cooldown	Endurance (1h)	-	**Endurance (1h)**	**Easy 1x90sec Intervall @10K pace (1h)**	**Q3 10K race @LT HR (1.5h)**
4	Easy (45min)	-	**Easy (1h)**	-	**Endurance (1h)**	**long Easy possibly slower (1,5h)**

Table 13: Example of build cycle including a Sunday 10K race in week 3.

What might be possible is to run six to eight kilometers at LT HR and see if LT pace drops. If it does not you might increase pace to 10K race pace. But if it does keeping LT pace up for the rest of the race might be challenging enough. If 10K races will be run once a week or multiple times during the build cycle it is advised to adjust race pace to not over stress the body. Table 14 shows the example for

80

LT pace of 4:15min/km which a runner can comfortably sustain for 30min. If a 10K run was attempted the pace is reduced to around 4:22min/km towards a finishing time of 43:40min/km. The pace reduction was based on Daniels' tables for a certain VO_2max and 20min of LT running (which Daniels uses as the standard time for an LT run). The paces that resulted from this approach (for the current example of 4:15min/km LT pace) would mean a pace of 4:24min/km for a 40min LT run. This is, in my experience, much too slow to have the same effect, the heart rate of the runner would not reach LT HR but would likely level off below. So I adjusted the concept by entering the current maximum time at LT pace before the pace decline was assumed. It is important to know whatever time the runner is used to running at LT pace. This represents basically the current LT training level. LT pace is then decreased using, in lieu of anything more sensible, the same curve used by Daniels (percentages can be used from table 14). In summary, an athlete has two options: he could just run the entire race at LT HR with the pace dropping beyond current LT training level or start at a lower estimated pace during the entire race altogether.

Duration [min]	30	35	40	45	50	55	60	65	70
Pace [min/km]	4:15	4:18	4:21	4:22	4:23	4:25	4:26	4:27	4:29
Distance [km]	7.1	8.1	9.2	10.3	11.4	12.5	13.5	14.6	15.6
Pace Reduction	0%	1.2%	2.2%	2.7%	3.3%	3.8%	4.3%	4.9%	5.5%

Table 14: Example adjustment of pace. 30min LT run can be run comfortably at 4:15. For longer runs, the pace needs to be adjusted accordingly.

Both methods are feasible, the first will be more taxing to the body but train LT more and the second will teach the body to cope with a more race-like experience of constant pace with increasing HR (admittedly not at an all out effort).

What the concepts around the build cycle show is that this cycle is much more subject to changes than the base cycle. One reason is that base endurance is developed inside a wide band of heart rates while effective LT training takes place in a narrower heart rate band. Also, in the build cycle the ratio between easy/endurance and running around LT pace is moved sharply towards the higher heart rates. This is very taxing which makes it difficult to fend off over the training week. Thus, build cycles should never be followed religiously as planned and need to be designed and adjusted for every individual runner.

An alternative setup of the build phase is the introduction of sub-LT running into it. Especially for 10K runners it is often hard to translate the new found LT pace towards a distance that might be twice as long as the regular LT run. On top of that, an increase in muscular endurance of such a magnitude can hardly be achieved during a couple of weeks of race preparation. Therefore, I personally like to introduce a variation of the build phase that suits my own needs very well. After the first build cycle according to tables 12 or 13 I focus the second build cycle on muscular endurance. This can be done as shown in table 15. The key workouts of this cycle is Q2 a 40min (9K) sub-LT run.

Week	Tue.	Wed.	Thu.	Fri.	Sat.	Sun.
1	Q1 warmup, 5x1K@LT pace 1min recovery, cooldown	Endurance 6 Hill Sprints (1h)	-	Q2 warmup, sub-LT (9K or 40min), cooldown	Endurance (1h)	Q3 long easy run with 10-20min LT at the end (2h)
2	Q1 warmup, 6x1K@10K race pace 1-2min recovery, cooldown	Endurance 2 Times Hill Circuit (1h)	-	Q2 warmup, sub-LT (9K or 40min), cooldown	Easy (1h)	Q3 long endurance (2h)
3	Q1 warmup, Fartlek with 10min LT HR + 10 min above LT with one hill and different paces, cooldown	Endurance (1h)	-	Q2 warmup, sub-LT to LT (9K or 40min), cooldown	Endurance (1h)	Q3 long easy run with 10-20min LT at the end (2h)
4	Easy (45min)	-	Easy (1h)	-	Recovery (slow) (45min-1h)	long Easy possibly slower (1,5h)

Table 15: Build cycle with focus on muscular endurance.

Although shown in table 15 as an identical workout the 9K sub-LT run should not be viewed as such. Q2 in week 3 is ideally a 9K LT run and weeks 1 and 2 progress towards this workout. The idea is to introduce a distance almost at a desired race distance (10K here) and increase pace over the cycle. Thus, a runner might start out at LT HR - 10 bpm in week 1, going to LT HR - 5 bpm and finally hitting LT HR. What this goal distance should be really depends on the runner and the goal distance of the season peak race. For the shown weekly load of around 6 hours and a goal 10K race a 9K tempo run is fine as it corresponds with a 40min run. For a much speedier runner a 9K might only be 30 min long which would obviously miss the point of this cycle adjustment. Especially if the season goal is a half marathon the distance will have to be longer. Then, the muscular endurance progression might be an hour long or even longer with the pace being adjusted accordingly. However, this cycle is extremely taxing as fatigue will definitely accumulate to a point where recovery is absolutely needed, a race during the recovery week is out of the question. Therefore, a runner has to find the maximum length of Q2 best suited for his needs. When in doubt, increasing the standard LT run (e.g. 6K in 25min) by 50% might just do the trick (9K and 40min in this example).

If advancing to a race cycle after this, it is important to take recovery at the end of this cycle seriously as one week of easy running might not even be enough. This is the downside of the muscular endurance heavy build cycle apart from injury risk. The upside is that a following prep/race cycle can focus on race specific paces much rather than muscular endurance which only needs maintenance.

4.5 Example training cycles different athletes train by

In this section, a small variety of build and prep/race cycles are introduced that different athletes have published online. The purpose is to show which different approaches athletes can take towards improving their running skills. Yet, many aspects of their training are similar and reflect the methods introduced in the previous chapters.

Table 16 shows a six week section of the training of the first athlete who we can classify as a hobby runner with a personal best 10K time of around 37 min. During the time the table covers the athlete ran multiple 10K or similar races at different efforts. On most days he runs easy runs of various lengths, mostly on flat surfaces, that vary in pace. Whether this variation is intended or occurs naturally during the runs is unknown. However, due to these variations in pace a shift between easy and endurance running pace is sometimes achieved. Adding this to the various lengths of the runs and the almost random distribution of runs during a week leads to the body hardly being able to adapt to the training cycle itself. Basic endurance should improve through this process. It is also visible that the runner is not a professional as the overall training volume is kept below eight hours a week.

Week	Mo.	Tue.	Wed.	Thu.	Fri.	Sat.	Sun.
1	Easy 1:40h	easy+ LT 4x1.6K (400m) 1:30h	easy 1:15h	-	easy 0:45h	-	easy 1h
2	easy long 2h	easy+LT 4x1K (400m) 1:30h	easy 0:50	easy 0:30	10K race (LT to 10K pace)	easy 0:30	10K race (10K pace)
3	easy 0:30	easy 1:30h	easy 0:50	easy 0:50	-	easy (1:10h) +10K(below LT) +easy (0:50)	-
4	easy long 2:00h	easy+LT 4x2K (400m) 1:30h	-	-	easy 1:20h	easy+ 3x1K @LT (400m)+ 2x1K(10K +above 10K) 1:30h	-
5	easy long 2:00h	-	easy 1:15h	easy 1:20h	-	-	easy 0:50
6	-	-	-	easy 1:30h	easy 1:15h	easy 1:15h	21.1km race (as long tempo run)

Table 16: Build cycle of example athlete A. Easy pace varies by about 15sec/min.

Note that Monday is mostly reserved for easy long runs, Tuesday seems to be interval training day. The interval training includes mostly LT pace intervals with recovery intervals run at easy pace, although in earlier training cycles not covered here faster 400m intervals are run. Before a race is run, e.g. during the second week, an easy run is used on the day before, strides seem to not be added to these.

Especially striking is the double 10K race in week two (Friday

85

and Sunday), both almost run at personal best pace. The four days after that serve as recovery days mostly.

Also quite interesting seems the Saturday run(s) in week three where the athlete runs over an hour to get to a race, then runs the race almost 30sec/km slower than the week before and adds another 50min of easy running at the end. A total of almost three hours of training are the result, a very heavy load for this athlete. In the case of this runner the races serve as tempo runs, which is quite common among non-elite runners. The interval runs are well known in 10K training plans, 4x1.6K and 4x2K are often found among runners, the Saturday LT intervals in week four introduce another race specific stimulus with the last two intervals leading towards 10K pace and even faster. Week five and six are mostly recovery weeks with week four being a bit of a compromise as training load is substituted for intensity. Therefore, it comes as no surprise that a sub-maximal half marathon is run on the Sunday of week 6. All in all, the training during this phase is very much an alternation between easy and LT running with races adding anaerobic stimulus. Following the conventions in this book, the phase shown in table 16 is still classified as a build cycle due to the continuation of build up workouts during the weeks after the races in week two.

A professional athlete would see quite a few deficits in the described plan: force and basic speed are not maintained or even progressed, no specific training on elevated easy towards endurance pace is done as well as the absence of anaerobic training. But, as athlete A is a hobby runner, the fun in running seems to be a key element in the training plan. And of course, easy running with slightly varying pace is the definition of recreational running. Over the years, it is still possible to achieve great race times (37min for a 10K is awesome!) without all the work that means enormous fatigue and injury risk.

Week	Mo.	Tue.	Wed.	Thu.	Fri.	Sat.	Sun.
1	easy (0:30)+ 7x600m(5K)with7x600m(LT)	1. easy(1h) 2. easy (0:30h)	easy (1:00h)	easy (0:20h)+ 7x100m Sprints(1-2m recovery)	easy (1:30h) with 100m elevation delta and increase towards LT	easy (0:50h) with 50m elevation delta	-
2	easy (0:30)+ 8x400m(1.5K)with 1min easy + 4x30sec(800m pace) with 1min easy	easy with 50m elevation delta 1:00h	1. easy towards endurance run 0:30h 2. easy 0:30h	easy (0:30h) + 10min LT+ 4x1min(1.5K pace increasing 10sec/km every interval) with below easy pace recovery	easy 1:00h	easy long with last 10min LT 2:00h	easy 1:00h
3	easy (0:30)+ 2x(2x800m@1.5K pace,300m @800m pace) with 2min below easy	easy 0:50h	easy with 30min increasing towards LT 1:00h	easy (possibly with drills) 0:30min	1. easy with 50m elevation delta 0:30h 2. easy 0:30h	easy 0:30h	below easy 0:30h + 1.5K race 0:35h
4	easy 1:00h	1. endurance (0:40h) 2. easy 0:35h	easy (0:30h) + 2x(1K,800m, 600m) paces unknown	easy 1:00h	1. easy (0:35h) 2. easy with 50m elevation delta (0:40h)	easy (0:30h) + 3.2K LT + 5x1min@1.5K pace with 1min below easy pace + 1.6K LT with	easy 1:00h
5	easy 0:15h + treadmill workout 0:50 (pace unknown)	easy with 50m elevation delta 1:00h	easy (0:20h) + 3x30sec@ 10K pace with 1min easy + 3x30sec @3K pace with 1min easy	1. easy with 50m elevation delta (0:30h) 2. easy (0:30h)	easy 0:20h	easy (0:30h) + unknown track workout	easy 1:15h

| 6 | 1. easy with 50m elevation delta (0:40h) 2. same as morning run | easy (0:30h) + 1.5K@LT + 5x300m@ 1.5K pace with 1:30min easy | 1. easy with 100m elevation delta (1:00h) 2. bike 1:00h | 1. easy with 50m elevation delta (0:45h) 2. easy with drills (0:30) | easy 0:30h | easy (0:30h) + 3K race | bike 1:15h |

Table 17: Prep/race cycle of example athlete B. easy pace varies by about 20sec/min.

Table 17 shows a whole different runner in comparison to athlete A. Athlete B trains professionally for 1500m and 3000m races, the table shows the prep/race cycle in the six weeks leading to a major 3K race. It is immediately recognizable that the training plan of athlete B includes more training load and much more intensity than anything athlete A would be even capable of. In all fairness, athlete B has a personal best of around 30min for the 10K and around 3:50min for the 1500m. During the first three weeks he progresses his interval training strictly towards his goal race of 1500m with 5K/LT intervals in week one, 1.5K/800m pace in week two and 1.5K/800m pace with extended interval lengths in week three. During week one, sprints and also some LT running is added to other runs with a general focus on endurance ans some force maintenance. Week two contains LT and 1.5K running in addition to the Monday interval session but making the intervals faster each time. This is a very good simulation of the last lap kick towards a strong finish in an already high paced 1500m race. Yet, one week before a 1500m race the two hour long run (with some LT running) is not missing as basic endurance needs to be maintained as well. The week before the first race is focused on easier running with the tempo run on Wednesday only slightly turning towards LT.

The second race in week six is approached in the same way. Intervals covering LT/1.5K pace in addition to faster paces in the first week (week 4). 10K/3K paces are trained in week 5 and LT/1.5K pace in week 6. These paces in connection with the 1500m race during week three is a sophisticated preparation for the goal race as the 1500m speed and lactate tolerance is maintained while more endurance is trained through focus on 10K and LT paces. This way the athlete can achieve fitness for both races or, to be more precise, take a step-by-step approach from fast and short towards longer and slower races. And indeed, two weeks (week 8, not shown) after the 3000m race a minor 8K cross country race is run and another in week 10.

What is a vital property of the plan of athlete B is constant changes to the plan. The body does not get used to a steady level of accumulated fatigue as the easy runs are distributed even by running two short easy runs in one day. The effect is that recovery through shorter runs is achieved as well as making sure that the body does not anticipate a certain workout pattern. On top of that, the individual needs of the specific runner are implemented into the plan which is the reason why no two plans are the same already on a semi-professional level like for athlete B. Also, training for short and fast races, the overall load is not much higher than for athlete A who is on a very different level. But the fatigue generated by elevated pace running is much higher.

Athlete C (German marathon runner Arne Gabius; www.arnegabius.de; Training Arne Gabius) is a professional marathon runner with personal bests of sub 2:10h for the marathon and sub 28min for the 10K. For convenience I will stay with the notation athlete C. The final 5 weeks before the season goal marathon are shown in table 18. Immediately it is recognized that the training load of up to 12h per week is significantly higher than for athlete B. As a rule of thumb, the longer the goal race distance the higher the weekly training load.

Week	Mo.	Tue.	Wed.	Thu.	Fri.	Sat.	Sun.
1	1. easy 0:40h	1. endurance 1:35h	1. easy 1:00h	1. easy 0:40h	1. easy 1:05h	Fartlek 10x2min+ 10x1min(1 min recovery)	
	2. easy 0:40h	2. easy + LT 0:15h	2. easy 1:00h	2. easy 1:20h	2. easy 0:45h		7K race
2	1. easy 1:00h	7K,6K,...,1K(1K recovery) from slightly below LT to 10K pace ca. 2:00h		easy 0:40h	easy + 7x2K@LT (4K recovery easy pace) 2:45h	-	1. easy 1:00h
	2. easy 1:00min		easy 1:20h				2. easy 0:40h
3	1. easy 0:45h	easy+ 12x1K@10K(1K easy recovery)	easy 0:45h	sub easy 10K recovery	1. easy 0:45h	-	1. 10K race (15sec below PB)
		2. hill sprints			2. easy 10K + hill sprints		2. easy 0:45h
4	easy 0:55h	endurance 0:35h	20K easy by feel	10K easy by feel	easy with last 15min LT 2:00h		endurance 0:40h
						easy 0:55min	
5	easy 0:45h		1. easy 0:40h		1. 6K sub easy	12K sub easy	easy + Marathon race (PB)
		easy+ Fartlek 10x2min+ 5x1min(1 min recovery) 1:15h	2. endurance 0:35h	8K sub easy	2. easy + hills 0:55h		

Table 18: Prep/race cycle of example athlete C (Arne Gabius,

www.arnegabius.de; **Training Arne Gabius)**. *Easy pace varies by about 20sec/min.*

Also, as this pro runner is on the verge of what is humanly possible, 12 hours of weekly load result in above 200km of running per week with the average pace being below 4min/km. Easy running is as fast as 3:45min/km and endurance running might be as fast as 3:30min/km. One hour of easy running is thus already more than 15K. On the one hand a 35min 10K run is still considered an easy run at conversational pace. On the other hand, 200km are 200km for tendons, muscles and joints making the pace and length of easy runs a delicate endeavor. Also, pro runners seem to have the tendency to run easy runs slightly slower than expected. This might be because their basic endurance can no longer be advanced and maintenance of this column is key. It might also be the case that the training load is just too high during this phase of training and additional stress from easy runs is to be avoided. No question, a very individual issue. In weeks 1 to 3 athlete C performs two Q sessions per week with lots of easy and some endurance running in mostly two runs per day. Significant is that all tempo sessions are done from slightly below LT to 10K pace with preparation races below or at 10K pace. The difference to a runner preparing for shorter races is that the tempo Q sessions are very long in comparison. For example, the week 2 Tuesday session which is a ladder workout starting with a 7K tempo run, then a 6K tempo run and so forth until the runner reaches a 1K tempo run with 1K easy rest intervals in between resulting in a total of almost 40K run during that session. This training load at that intensity is almost unthinkable even for a sub-elite runner. But this session tells the elite runner all he needs to know about the possible outcome of the race weeks later as he is then confident to be able to hold the high pace of a marathon for a long time. Only three days after the epic ladder workout an over-distance run is done meaning almost 50K of running in under three hours. Athlete C can now almost be sure to be able to achieve a great marathon time as long as the rest of the plan works out (and whether he can put it into practice on race day as well!)

In addition, the pace used for the Q sessions is directly supporting future marathon pace. The supporting pace is LT pace. In this case a marathon might be run at around 3:05min/km, LT might be at around 2:55min/km and 10K pace at around 2:50min/km. Thus, the runner uses a lot of LT pace running in different formats with some 10K running to help muscular endurance. Marathon pace itself is (almost) not trained for an elite runner which might be different for the hobby runner. The elite runner always to some extent gambles with the "did not finish" label while hobby runners might run endurance runs for 42.2K. If the hobby runner fails to achieve his goal he just finishes with a slower time while the elite might not be able to finish at all.

Weeks 4 and 5 are tapering weeks for athlete C where training load and intensity are reduced step by step. Running by feel takes away the pressure to perform. Many runners run tapering runs too fast and thus destroy their race day performance. This is especially true because easy running might be slower at the usual easy HR due to fatigue. Still, the final long run is executed just nine days before the race at what I might call endurance pace (38K in 2h). Two days before the race, a slight stimulus for the muscles is introduced, in this case hill running (surges or sprints might do as well depending on the runner). The day before the race is a 12K easy run which might be around 45min of time long. This sounds familiar to what athlete A and B are doing the day before a race, something to keep in mind.

What becomes clear when comparing these three example runners is that race day preparation can turn out to be very different. Of course this depends on knowledge of the individual who designed the plan giving advantage to the pro runners who are able to rely on world class coaches. Also, for the hobby athlete, running a fun event might take precedence over the optimum preparation. Another aspect is that the goal event demands very different race specific workouts. The marathon runner relies on keeping up the speed side of his abilities with LT workouts and 10K races with extensive volume while the 3K runner focuses on 1500m pace and LT running generally being able to endure much less volume. The bottom line is that many factors influence other(!) people's training plan. Simply copying such a plan makes little to no sense as the individual needs for those runners may be very different from your own.

4.6 The peak and race cycles

From analysis of sample athletes' prep/race cycles it was possible to derive the need for adaption to the goal race much more so than during base and build cycles. Obviously, the closer a runner approaches a goal event the more race specific the workouts need to be.

One general rule as to how to do this is the duration of the goal event. The longer the race will take, the longer prep/race cycles also need to be. This relationship is best explained using time of adaption to stimuli. The longest adaption is needed for duration itself. For a marathon race for example the volume of the long run is increased over weeks. The shorter the run an athlete is used to the longer this adaption will take. Generally, the cycle is somewhere between 8 and 12 weeks long (6-10 weeks of increasing long run volume with 2 weeks of tapering). For a fast race (say a 5K race) this time is reduced to 4-6 weeks (3-5 weeks with 1 week of tapering).

5K	-	Q1 1.25h AE, S, LT	Easy 1h E	-	Q2 1.25h LT+AE, (E)	Easy 1h E	Q3 1.5h E+LT+AE
Marathon	-	Q1 0.5h S, LT	Easy 1-2h E	-	Q2 1h LT, (E)	Easy 0.5h E	Q3 2-3h E, (LT)

Table 19: Prep Cycles for different race events and 6h weekly running. AE: Anaerobic endurance; S: Speed; E:Endurance column; LT: Lactate threshold.

Table 19 shows possible different approaches to a 5K and a marathon race prep/race cycle. For the former, endurance (column), LT and speed need to be maintained while anaerobic endurance can be build over the course of a few weeks and is therefore pronounced. For the marathon, speed and LT are maintained while the length of Q3 has to approach around 35K with some of that being at race pace. For a hobby runner running the marathon below his ability (actually closer to being a very long endurance run) the entire preparation could be geared towards endurance pace. The difference shows that it seems rather impossible to advance all race specific abilities at the same time. It is necessary to choose to maintain some abilities and progress a few race specific ones.

The race specific requirements force the athlete to apply a plan that addresses the needs of the particular race. The training plans that are readily available on the Internet reflect this as they usually cover the last weeks before a race only. These plans are really peak/race cycle plans and can be found for the popular race distances. All in all, they are more or less well designed and would actually help the athlete to achieve his race goal. But the prefabricated plans do not take the following into account:

1. The specific needs of the athlete in question,
2. the training carried out before the race specific plan is begun,
3. the specific properties of the race itself (e.g. hilly course).

Reason 1. is important as the prep/race cycle needs to be as personal as possible but reason 2. is crucial because even a perfect plan is going to fail if the necessary prerequisites are not present. For example, without a sufficient endurance base the race specific development is always going to fail. The third reason is important for a few races namely with hills, unknown surfaces (e.g. trails), technical passages (e.g. climbing across stones) or other aspects that need to be practiced. The most common aspect in the third category is food/drink intake during long races.

The first step is therefore to develop a generic prep/race cycle for a specific target race (much like the plans one finds online). For this, it is necessary to ask what race specific abilities have to be present to perform well? For extreme examples this is easy to answer. Most people would agree that the ability to sprint all out towards the finish line has a minor effect on the performance in a marathon while a very highly developed endurance column is not decisive for a 400m race. But how about other training columns? To circumvent such theoretical analysis the idea of specificity was introduced and can be found in many publications. I personally like the introduction by Brad Hudson and Matt Fitzgerald ("Running Faster"). Specificity means that the closer an athlete approaches a goal race the more his training has to reflect the requirements of the race in question. A marathon runner extends the long run each week towards 35km while approaching goal race pace. In this case, what the authors call direct support paces are trained. These paces are generally the paces neighboring to race pace.

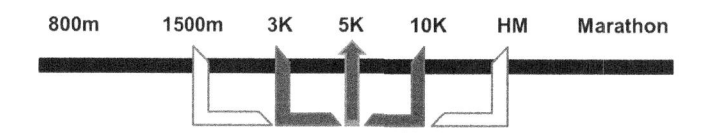

Fig 13: Direct (solid) and indirect (transparent) support paces for a 5K example race.

Fig. 13 shows the race paces most relevant for the current discussion. The two race paces faster and slower compared to goal race pace are important to focus on during the prep/race cycle. They deliver direct support for the race in question. For example, training for a 5K race, intervals will begin with 1500m and progress towards 3K race pace with a likely 5K test race integrated into the cycle. Tempo runs will include half marathon pace first and should progress towards 10K pace. This progression can be done in many ways, applying 10-15min intervals at first HM and then 10K pace (as Brad Hudson suggests) or steady state 9K runs at sub-LT pace (first week at HM, next week at LT pace) with progression towards 10K pace. As 5K pace is faster than LT pace (up to 20sec/km faster) both the interval progression as well as the tempo run progression conclude at 5K pace. A very common workout around 10 days before the 5K goal race is then a workout with 5x1K@5K-pace with 1-2min recovery jogs between intervals sometime followed by a 1K at 3K pace to add a speed component. This final workout lets the runner know if the goal race pace is generally achievable. For a 10K race this workout would be 4x2K@10K pace(1-2min recovery) and for a half marathon it would be 6x1600m@HM-pace(1.5-2min recovery) for relatively slow runners and up to 3x5K@HM-pace (1.5min recovery) for the pro runner.

Obviously, if a runner trains for a 1500m race he needs 800m and 400m paces as support paces as well. On the other end of the pace spectrum, if training for a marathon, the next slower support pace is likely around endurance pace. Endurance and easy paces are trained at anyway in any training plan which excludes them from being specifically called support paces. Therefore, there are no support paces slower than marathon pace. Yet, this scenario makes clear that the marathon needs a very solid endurance (and base cycle) foundation. The idea for its preparation is to transfer speed, acquired through 10K or even 5K races, to the longer distances of half marathon and finally the marathon. This explains why in almost every training plan a preparation half marathon is placed around a month before the goal marathon with the signature long run (anywhere from 35K at easy pace for beginners to 15km at easy plus 20K at marathon pace for pro runners) planned two weeks before the goal race.

Now that we know the signature workouts it is necessary to calculate backwards to the current state of training. Often times, the goal race is on a fixed day so the time line is defined as well. Generally, the faster race pace is the shorter the prep cycle can be. 4 weeks for a 5K and anything faster, 8 weeks for 10K and 12 weeks for half marathon and marathon races are general guidelines to go by. But the time an athlete needs to prepare for a specific race needs to be found out on an individual bases. So let us assume an athlete went through several base (say three) and build (say two) cycles. The endurance, power and speed columns are well developed but not much running was done at lactate heavy paces up to this point. A beginner to medium runner could now perform reasonably well in a race ranging from 5K to a half marathon but a top performance will only be possible if race specificity is the focus of the prep cycle.

This reasoning is especially true if shorter races are attempted since paces faster than 5K race pace are omitted in base and even build cycles. Yet, I find it fascinating that the entire racing fitness for a short race can be built in as little as a couple of weeks after essentially 5 months of endurance heavy training.

4.6.1 The 5K prep/race cycle

The main focus of the 5K-specific prep cycle is the evolution of weekly intervals towards 5K pace as well as maintenance of endurance (both basic and towards LT pace). Table 20 goes once again back to the familiar 6h training week example. It shows that Tuesday intervals (Q1) focus on 1.5K (or mile) pace (week 1), 3K pace (week 2), 3K+5K pace (week 3) and 5K pace in week 4. Q2 on Fridays is designed under the assumption that the build cycle contained quite a bit of longer sub-LT and LT running. The result of this aspect is two-fold: first, muscular endurance (running at high pace for a long time) is developed past the 5K mark while the athlete feels quite exhausted from this preceding training cycle. Therefore, Friday tempo runs are kept to the lower end of the spectrum concerning training load, with 5K at half marathon pace (week 1), 2 times 3K between half marathon and 10K pace (week 2) and two 5K runs between half marathon and 10K pace (week 3 and 4). Again, as with all training suggestions presented here, it is assumed that a 5K run at 10K pace does not take longer than 25 minutes.

Week	Tue.	Wed.	Thu.	Fri.	Sat.	Sun.
1	8-12x400m@1.5K (3min recovery)	easy 1:00h + 3x8sec sprints	-	5K sub-LT (HM pace)	easy 1:00h	easy 1.5h with 2-3K@10K at the end
2	5-6x800m@3K (3min recovery)	easy 1:00h	-	2x3K LT (HM -10K pace) 2min easy recovery	1x90sec@5K 3min recovery at easy pace 1:00h	5K test race
3	5x800m@5K 1min Recov+1-2x400m@3K (3minRecov)	easy 1:00h + 3x8sec sprints	-	5K LT (HM-10K pace)	easy 1:00h	easy 1.5h
4	5x1K@5K (1-2min recovery easy pace)	easy 1:00h + 3x8sec sprints	-	5K LT (HM-10K pace)	easy 1:00h	-
5	5x90sec@5K 3min recovery at easy pace or Easy	4x90sec@5K 3min recovery at easy pace	3x90sec@5K 3min recovery at easy pace	-	1x90sec@5K 3min recovery at easy pace	5K race

Table 20: 5K prep and race cycle(week 5). Note: every run faster than easy pace is preceded by 15min warm up and followed by 15min cool down.

In the weeks prior to this cycle, LT pace presented the maximum pace the runner was training at. Therefore, higher paced running with some work above LT, meaning in the anaerobic regime, is needed to prepare for the 5K race. The muscles need to get used to the 5K distance and some lactic acid. Yet, Q1 and Q3 during these weeks introduce a stress that should not be neglected. The athlete should be careful not to run these runs too fast for the reason of increased fatigue. This is also the reason why Q2 is vaguely defined as half marathon to 10K pace as it depends on how fresh the athlete feels on the one hand. Also, a run beginning with half marathon pace and slowly working towards 10K pace will add the psychological element of a negative split. Week 2 is a compromise especially pronounced by the LT run (Q2) as 2x3K can be seen rather as the maximum for this week. The first 3K can probably be run at LT pace while it is very possible that the next 3K turn out to be cut for a 2K because the run feels too hard. The test race in week 2 (Q3) is the important workout of the week and should be attempted around 5sec/km slower than goal race pace as fatigue will make it harder to achieve a goal race equivalent result. Yet, this workout is key to understanding how realistic the race goal really is. Many runners prepare well but have unrealistic aspirations for the race in question. If an athlete begins the test race 5sec/km below goal race pace and still slows down 5-10sec/km (or more) the race target for the goal race should be adjusted. The reason is that the weekly interval runs (Q1) will blur the picture of current race fitness. Intervals can often be finished at the intended pace according to the training plan but the effort can not be sustained for the entire race distance. The athlete with sufficient base and build cycle training will on the other hand have a clear view of LT pace (and LT HR) making 10K and 5K race pace somewhat more realistically predictable. But there is always doubt, the variance resulting from this is about 5sec/km in my experience.

Another issue could be that after lengthy base and build phases the runner is simply not used to higher pace racing (especially the case when alactic sprinting is neglected). Therefore, he might not be able to endure 5k-5sec/km pace for the entire length of the race. An indicator is that HR stays comparably low but the test race feels too taxing. In this case, Q2 during the following weeks 3 and 4 can be attempted with some 5K pace in the middle of the run. The run might begin with 1K@LT-pace followed by increased pace running including some 5K pace running. This kind of training, though it is already very close to race effort and therefore quite taxing, prepares the mental side of racing very well. A runner might have the physical ability to run a certain race but is simply afraid of the new pace. If recovery time still works out for the runner these tempo runs are very effective to provide stimulus as well as confidence in his own abilities. The downside is obvious: too much race effort might lead to a tired or even injured athlete on race day. For those who would like to attempt this form of race preparation, the following setups for Q2 are practical for the 5K run (pace for each kilometer):

- LT - LT - 10K - 10K - 5K
- LT - 5K - LT - 5K - 10K

- LT - 10K - 5K - 5K - LT or 10K

Each of these workouts has the point of getting used to race effort and also training the body to use the produced lactic acid as fuel.

Following the test race, week 3 has the general role of a (pseudo-)recovery week, further progression of LT running may or may not be omitted and the intervals leave an option for less work at the end. All-in-all, week 3 will probably feel quite taxing so the longer run on Sunday (Q3) is somewhat optional and can be reduced in duration if needed. Week 4 contains the signature workout before the race where recovery between the intervals should ideally be one minute in length and run at easy pace. The reason for this is that many runners feel confident about their abilities by finishing this workout with 5 intervals exactly at race pace but they have to walk at least between the interval 4 and 5 if not most intervals. This strongly indicates that the selected race pace is too much at the current training level. The recovery portion at easy running tempo will show if interval 5 is possible with a reasonable heart rate (above LT HR but nowhere near the maximum should be a guideline to follow).

Week 5 then introduces something that has not been mentioned before: the race cycle itself. Studies have shown that the week prior to a race is best used for tapering. Training load is reduced but intensity is kept high. Different methods to do this have been mentioned in literature. I prefer the cycle mentioned by Joe Friel who quotes a study about 1500m runners and their significant improvement due to this one week alone. The idea is that every day approaching the goal race one interval less is run. In combination with 15mins warm up and cool down at easy pace this leaves the final run at 32 minutes and the first run still in under one hour. In combination with Q3 in week 4 being a rest day this should present a reasonable preparation for the race.

Of course, different race cycles are possible and often applied. Athlete A (table 16) uses three easy runs before a halfmarathon race, athlete B (table 17) runs 0:30h easy runs before 1500m and 3K races as well as easy runs including hills two and three days before a race. Athlete C (table 18) takes a similar approach as athlete B to his marathon race preparation with a slow jog below easy pace the day before the race and easy running also including hills on the days before that.

4.6.2 The 10K prep cycle

For the 10K race, a philosophy (table 21) similar to the 5K prep/race cycle is employed.

Week	Tue.	Wed.	Thu.	Fri.	Sat.	Sun.
1	4x800m@3K+4x400m1.5K (3min easy recovery)	easy 1:00h + 3x8sec sprints	-	9K sub-LT (HM pace)	easy 1:00h	easy 1.5h
2	6-8x800m@5K (3min easy recovery)	easy 1:00h + 3x8sec sprints	-	2x4K sub-LT (HM/LT pace) with 2min easy recovery	easy 0:30h	1.5h easy with 2-3K@10K at the end
3	6x1K@5K (3min easy recovery)	easy 1:00h	-	2x3K LT (HM-10K pace) 2min easy recovery	easy 0:30h	5K test race
4	4x1.6k@10-5K (2-3min easy recovery)	easy 1:00h	-	6-8K LT (HM-10K pace)	easy 1:00h	easy 1.5h
5	4x2K@10K (1-2min recovery)	easy 1:00h	-	6-8K LT (HM-10K pace)	easy 1:00h	-
6	5x90sec@10K 3min recovery at easy pace or easy	4x90sec@10K 3min recovery at easy pace	3x90sec@10K 3min recovery at easy pace	-	1x90sec@10K 3min recovery at easy pace	10K race

Table 21: 10K prep and race cycle(week 6). Note: every run faster than easy pace is preceded by 15min warm up and followed by 15min cool down.

Just as for the shorter race, Q1 (Tuesday) is advanced from 1.5K/3K towards 10K race pace while LT runs are increased in speed towards the goal race pace. The test race again is a 5K race to emphasize support pace. How to deal with Q2 (Friday) is a little tricky however. If sufficient muscular endurance was build in the training cycles directly prior to the 10K prep cycle shorter LT runs could be undertaken especially during week 1,2 and 4 if recovery is needed. However, 10K race specificity is 10K pace on the one hand but also a great endurance base including muscular endurance is needed. Therefore, I generally find 7-9K LT runs practical with a strong finish as a simulation for the race in question. In contrast to other authors (e.g. Jack Daniels) who include LT runs far below race duration I like to approach this specific duration as closely as possible. The obvious downside to this approach is the accumulation of fatigue that might hinder race day performance. Thus, the very taxing weeks 2 and 3 should be counteracted with less taxing, yet more specific, weeks 4 and 5. Q2 (Friday) during these two weeks need to be adjusted according to individuals level of fatigue. This means that Q2 in weeks 4 and 5 could have to be ended significantly before the 8K mark is reached. This depends on the preconditioning of the runner: is muscular endurance an issue or does the pace push the athlete into the anaerobic regime too soon? The former can still somewhat be dealt with in week 4 and 5 but the later can only be answered with a reduced race pace altogether. However, for an athlete who carried out e.g. three base and two build cycles it is very common that muscular endurance is lacking at this point. For this athlete, the longer LT runs will help prepare for the race.

In addition, 5K and 10K prep/race cycles are linked through 5K races serving as preparation races for both events. Therefore, many runners either run the 5K prep race for their 10K preparation already to achieve a personal best or they add a 10K prep cycle to the end of the 5K cycle. If the latter is done, it might be difficult to maintain basic and/or muscular endurance, a specific week or two to emphasize these abilities might then be in order. If the athlete feels no need for such an intermission, weeks 4 to 6 of the 10K prep/race cycle can easily be added as weeks 7 to 9 to the cycle presented in table 20 to race first a 5K and then a 10K. This method was practically employed by athlete B (from 1500m to 3K racing it works similarly) in the above discussion of real life prep cycles (table 17). After such a race combination, I would recommend going back to at least one base cycle and possible one build cycle to return to peak fitness concerning the basic columns.

Another possibility would be that it was found that muscular endurance was a problem for the 5K race. To add a 10K prep cycle after a 5K prep/race cycle would then be somewhat of an issue. Then, muscular endurance will for sure be a focus for the 10K race cycle. As the result, the adjusted 10K cycle could look something like in table 22.

Week	Tue.	Wed.	Thu.	Fri.	Sat.	Sun.
0	...	...	...	...	...	5K race
1	easy 0:45-1:00h or rest	easy 1:00h	-	9K sub-LT run	easy to recovery 0:45-1:00h	easy 1-1.5h
2	4x1.6k@10K (1-2min easy recovery)	easy 1:00h	-	7-9K LT (HM-10K pace)	easy to recovery 0:45-1:00h	easy 1-1.5h
3	4x2K@10K (1-2min recovery)	easy 1:00h	-	8-9K LT (HM-10K pace)	easy to recovery 0:45-1:00h	-
4	easy 0:45-1:00h	4x90sec@10K 3min recovery at easy pace or easy	3x90sec@10K 3min recovery at easy pace	-	1x90sec@10K 3min recovery at easy pace	10K race

Table 22: Adjusted 10K prep/race cycle following a 5K peak race with muscular endurance constraints.

Week 0 is the final week of the 5K prep/race cycle with the peak race on Sunday. Week 1 is first of all governed by the need for recovery from the race. The recovery is short (2-3 days at most) but Q1 has to be changed to an easy run or even a rest day for most athletes. Q2 will then, for all weeks, focus on a run almost at race length. Week 1 will introduce the new distance at a moderate pace below LT, say somewhere between HM and LT pace. The next day will then have to be a recovery day otherwise the accumulated

103

fatigue will build from week to week until the race. The long run on Sunday should be cut short if fatigue is too high. Remember, this phase of training is designed to maintain basic endurance if at all. Many runners may feel this running column to deteriorate because of the anaerobic running during the intervals. For the upcoming interval session in Q1 a slight change might be helpful as well. We can safely assume that the runner is in peak shape for his 5K race. Therefore, the 4x1.6K intervals of week 2 do not need to lean towards 5K race pace but rather towards 10K race pace. But then, it is necessary to cut recovery short as muscular endurance is in focus. Basically, more running close to race pace with less recovery will keep the heart rate elevated and the muscles will stay exhausted (at least enough to cause adaption). Yet, lactic acid will be dealt with during the easy paced recovery. It is then recommended to maybe begin with a 1 minute recovery jog and increase recovery as needed. A great workout would be to run all intervals at 10K pace with at least the first two recovery runs limited to 1 minute. The final interval could increase towards 5K race pace. The same happens in week 3 where interval length is increased and recovery should be limited to 1 minute.

To deal with the issue of muscular endurance weeks 2 and 3 are critical. Ideally, the 9K run of week one could be repeated at LT pace which puts a lot of stress on the body. It could also be possible to run 5-6K at LT pace and then increase to 10K race pace. If the workout has to be cut short after 7K because muscles hurt too much that is another hint for lacking muscular endurance. It might then be a good idea to interrupt for 1-2 minutes with easy running and add another 2K at LT pace. The weekend will then again be devoted to recovery, a short jog on Saturday and maybe 1h of easy running on Sunday. Week 3 is a gamble though. 10K specific intervals are needed to get as race specific as possible. Q2 on other hand could be a 9K HM run if fatigue is too great. But if the runner is able to run 2-4K at 10K pace, and maybe being able to alternate between LT and 10K race pace during Q2, he is very well prepared. But recovery during race week is key. Tuesday will then definitely be devoted to recovery and maybe even Wednesday before the race.

What I tried to introduce is that no two athletes have the same requirements towards the prep/race cycle. For the intermediate runner, in contrast to pro runners, the individual weaknesses might be unclear. The prep cycles will reveal them though if an athlete pays attention. Having an issue with muscle pain at low heart rate during LT runs (muscular endurance)? Heart rate rises into the anaerobic (base endurance lacking, adjust goal)? These and other questions should be asked and the prep/race cycle can be adjusted to at least reduce the negative effect resulting from the specific issue.

4.6.3 The half marathon prep/race cycle

The half marathon, as well as the marathon later in this chapter, I would divide into two separate approaches to racing and thus also to training for it:

1. A pace close or at endurance run pace for the more relaxed approach e.g. to run a minor race or,
2. the achievement of a personal best run at the designated half marathon pace.

I personally favor the first approach over the second one as it basically guarantees enjoying the race. Especially during scenic races or races with lots of hills (where a PB is not achievable anyway) this approach is very positive in my eyes. I e.g. used it to prepare for the Wings for Life World Run 2016 where I finished after 29km at endurance pace. The run took place on an enjoyable course with temperatures unusually high for what I was used to. My pulse was elevated by about 10bpm, still I was able to execute my race plan due to the lower pace I had planned for in the first place.

For this endurance run based prep/race cycle (table 23) we again assume 2-3 base cycles and at least one build cycle. The reason one build cycle is omitted is that the preparation for an endurance pace based race is practically a modified build cycle in itself. It could in turn be used to prepare for a marathon race right afterwards.

In table 23, a race preparation with a high emphasis on the endurance side is shown. In weeks 1 – 3, all Q-runs are simultaneously advanced: 10K race pace intervals, LT runs and of course the long run. For many runners, all long runs exceed the half marathon distance by a couple of kilometers. This is especially true for the endurance long run in week 2 which came out as 24km for my preparation. Of course, this makes little sense if a half marathon was the sole goal. But if a runner would enter a marathon prep/race cycle right after these three weeks would make a lot of sense.

Week	Tue.	Wed.	Thu.	Fri.	Sat.	Sun.
1	easy 1:00h	Endurance + 4x1K@LT 1min recovery at easy 1:00h	-	6K LT	endurance 1:00h	Easy + 2-3K LT 2:00h
2	Endurance + 5x1K@10K 1-2min recovery at easy 1:00h	Endurance 1:00h	-	7K LT	easy 1:00h	Endurance 1:55h
3	Fartlek with 3-5L pace and hills 1:00h	Endurance 1:00h	-	easy 1:00h	recovery 1:00h	Easy 2:00h
4	Moderate Fartlek with some Tempo at LT and hills	-	Easy 0:50h	-	recovery 0:45h	Endurance 1:20h
5	Easy (0:45-1:00h)	4x90sec@HM 3min recovery at easy pace	3x90sec@HM 3min recovery at easy pace	-	1x90sec@HM 3min recovery at easy pace	HM Race @endurance pace

Table 23: Half marathon prep/race cycle for a race run at endurance pace. All runs faster than endurance pace include 15min warm up and cool down.

Also, like in my case, the goal race had around 30km of distance which is well prepared with a 24km run at race pace three weeks before the event. What is relevant for whoever tackles a half marathon for the first time, this preparation also works if somewhere between endurance and half marathon pace was the goal for the event. Looking at this in terms of an example, HM-pace might be around 4:30min/km with endurance pace at around 4:50min/km. A reasonable approach could be to try running the event at 4:40min/km and maybe add a tempo run up to LT HR at the end of the race (if possible). For a first timer, this might take care of the psychological element of the new challenge as well as the uncertainty of the new distance.

Of course, if a personal best is the goal for the event, a whole different approach needs to be taken. Then, the long run will advance only to around the half marathon distance with much more emphasis on speed endurance, muscular endurance and LT endurance development. Again, I am an advocate for training that leads close to race specific runs which would be a long run leading towards race pace. An example could be 10km endurance pace plus 10km HM pace or a progression run starting out after 10km of endurance running and progressing even to 10K pace. For athletes who can manage such a long run inside a training cycle, the final interval workout would be up to 3x5K@HM-pace(1.5min recovery) while the intermediate runner might use 6x1600m@HM-pace(1.5-2min recovery) as his final workout of that sort. A good compromise is a run with 3x4km at HM pace with 1.5min recovery, In any case, we are talking about a runner here who does not deplete his glycogen stores during a half marathon (events significantly shorter than 2 hours). This is important as a half marathon can then consist of a pace that predominantly lies outside the fat burning range (even close to LT pace for pro runners).

Table 24 shows a significant change comparing to table 23 as much more running at higher paces is introduced. The first three weeks of the cycle increase accumulated fatigue significantly, some runners might even have to skip a workout because it is too much at this point. However, week 4 and 5 will lead to a transformation of the muscle fatigue towards enhanced muscular endurance. Assuming a runner is able to perform well in a 10K and wishes to also perform well in a half marathon race the challenge is to endure a marginally slower pace for more than twice the distance. To achieve this, a large load of muscle fatigue due to long fast pace running is to be accumulated and again relieved through sufficient recovery.

Week	Tue.	Wed.	Thu.	Fri.	Sat.	Sun.
1	5x1K@5K 1-2min recovery at easy 1:00h	Easy 1:00h	-	9K sub-LT	Easy to recovery 1:00h	Easy 2:00h
2	6x1.6K@10K 1-2min recovery at easy 1:30h	Easy 1:00h	-	7K LT	Easy to recovery 1:00h	Easy + Endurance 2:00h
3	6x2K@HM 1-2min recovery at easy 1:30h	Easy 1:00h	-	8K LT (or Easy if too fatigued) 1:00	Easy to recovery 1:00h	Endurance + progression run towards HM pace 2:00h
4	Easy 1:00h	3x5K@HM-pace 1.5min recovery at easy pace 1:30h	-	Easy 1:00h	recovery 0:30h	Endurance + 10K HM pace 2:00
5	Moderate Fartlek with some Tempo at LT and hills 1:00h	-	Easy 0:50h	-	recovery 0:45h	Endurance 1:30h
6	Easy (0:45-1:00h)	4x90sec@HM 3min recovery at easy pace	3x90sec@HM 3min recovery at easy pace	-	1x90sec@HM 3min recovery at easy pace	HM Race @HM pace

Table 24: Prep/race cycle for a PB goal half marathon. All runs faster than endurance pace include 15min warm up and cool down.

In the end, it is not important if every run can be carried out as described as the stimulus is what counts, the above plan represents somewhat a maximum of what is possible for most. But even if the progression run in week 3 ends with 1:45h of endurance running and 15min of HM pace running and the following interval in week 4 falls short with only 2x5km+1x3km at HM pace, the stimulus is large. In effect, the longer the event, the less I am a proponent of executing the plan as designed. Of course, setting up a 8x400m@3K type interval should probably be forced to endure the last interval to the end. But longer distance plans work through accumulation of fatigue

108

which in turn is hard to predict. Thus, I design plans that are often a bit too taxing just to reduce them to what is needed. The body, much more so than for short and fast paced intervals, tells an athlete how much is actually too much. The key is to extend sub-LT, LT, or HM-paced running to a longer distance as usual.

Cycle	Standard Approach	Alternative Approach
1	Base 1	Base 1
2	Base 2	Base 2
3	Base 3	Base 3
4	Build 1	Prep/Race endurance pace
5	Build 2	Build 1
6	Prep/Race (Either endurance or PB HM)	Prep/Race (PB HM)

Table 25: Approaches to training cycle design for half marathon races.

All in all, such a plan will only work if the foundation is set accordingly (compare table 25). This means base cycles with sufficient long running, followed by at least one build cycle for the PB half marathon are needed before the prep/race cycle can be begun. Alternatively, the first build cycle can be replaced with the prep/race cycle for an endurance paced half marathon, followed by a regular build cycle and a PB-pace prep/race cycle. This second approach will place a strong emphasis on the endurance side of half marathon running especially interesting for the less experienced runners who might feel that HM-pace is an ambitious goal at that particular point.

4.6.4 The marathon prep/race cycle

The marathon is in many ways a special case. For all other races it is somewhat possible to estimate the outcome by looking at the training weeks prior. LT pace and HR, easy pace etc. lead to a conclusion about a possible race pace window. The marathon however possesses an implicit uncertainty that is based on the fact that training every aspect of the race is simply impossible.

It is however possible to lay the foundation of a successful marathon by establishing easy and endurance paces, strength and basic speed in the base cycles. The corresponding LT pace and muscular endurance is emphasized in the build phase while the basic abilities are maintained. Then, the purpose of the prep cycle is to extend the running abilities towards marathon distance. The problem is two fold. First, it is not possible to train marathon paced running all the way up to 40km distance or so because fatigue would be too great and would impair the following training. Second, the marathon requires a time of more than 2.5 hours for intermediate runners (mostly more than 3 hours). As glycogen stores only last for up to two hours emphasis is placed on fat metabolism beyond a certain distance. Therefore, in theory, a runner might have trained the appropriate paces and extended the distance but simply runs out of fuel typically beyond the 30km mark. This is what is often described as hitting the wall, a very unpleasant experience. If fat metabolism at marathon race pace is unknown (it can be measured) at least the fueling strategy has to be sufficient during a race. A more comfortable approach is to increase the maximum duration of the longest race over the years to approach the marathon slowly and as the result without suffering. As in the previous chapters, the training for a marathon in terms of the prep/race cycle is discussed. Unlike for the shorter races the fueling strategy is of additional importance.

One of the results of these aspects is that existing marathon training plans have different goals as well as different aspects of previous training in mind. The resulting plans are therefore vastly different (although with some underlying similarities). To ease into the key elements I found it helpful how successful coaches approached the subject in the past.

Daniels ("Daniels' Running Formula") introduces several training plans. Among them is an 18 week plan with two Q-sessions per week, The rest of the week is either easy running or rest. Daniels' proposes to advance the long run from 25 to 36 km and introduces add-ons after a while. In fact, an alternation between an easy long run with more distance, a shorter long run advancing the length of marathon paced running and an easy long run with add-ons is introduced. Additionally, Daniels' proposes LT runs about every other to every week and some 3K and 5K intervals every 4 weeks.

Brad Hudson ("Running Faster") introduces a significantly more complex system. He divides a 20 week training plan into several blocks. The first six weeks are devoted to advancing the long run from 19 to 29km. He proposes to alternate easy long runs and progression runs where during the final 20 to 30 minutes the pace is increased towards some medium pace. Also Fartleks (3K pace) and hill repetitions are present. Week 7 to 10 of Brad Hudson's plan show the first marathon paced runs, some 10K tempo running, 5K and 10K intervals as well as weekly LT runs. In weeks 11 to 14 the long run will be again advanced, to 32km now. These weekly easy long runs are again alternated with progression runs. Additional marathon and 10K pace runs fill the training week with some LT running and 3K and 5K intervals. A half marathon race at marathon pace is part of week 15. Week 16 to 19 are similar to week 11 to 14 with the long run being again advanced towards 37 km and the marathon paced runs include up to 29km of marathon pace (a clear sign that highly trained individuals are the target audience). The faster paces between 3K and 10K are maintained with ladder intervals, LT pace is as well maintained through shorter runs. Shorter marathon paced runs complete the week. Week 20 is tapering for the race in week 21.

Pete Pfitzinger ("Advanced Marathoning") on the other hand presents an 18 week plan. He breaks the plan down into four sections: endurance, LT+endurance, race prep and taper plus race. Weeks 1 to 6 (endurance) focus on the increase of all distances: easy runs towards 16km, LT runs from 6 to 8km and long runs from 19 to 26km. Also, marathon pace is already present in the longest runs. Week 7 to 11, "endurance and LT", advances the long run farther to 32km and also the marathon pace portion to up to 19km. Just like in the phase before LT runs are introduced almost every week. Some

5K intervals are also found. Weeks 12 to 15, "race preparation", show some 5K intervals increasing from 5x600m towards 4x1200m. Also, 8 to 15K tuneup races are introduced twice. The long run is again increased to a maximum of 32 km three weeks before the race. Marathon paced running has a maximum of 23km five weeks before the race (somewhat on the upper end of what an intermediate runner would be capable of). Weeks 16 to 18, "taper and race", introduce some 5K intervals (5x600m and 8x100m) and an 8 to 10K tuneup race 2 weeks before the goal event. Also, the distance of the long run decreases from 26 to 19km.

Many other marathon plans exist with different approaches in each one of them. The plans mentioned above show this well. They also somewhat reflect the evolution of training concepts as well as who the typical runner is who trains according to these plans. Daniels' e.g. worked mainly with athletes who ran competitively for years already. His runners had strong cross country and/or track backgrounds. For them, the increase in distance of the long run while maintaining speed and power was probably a key element.

Brad Hudson coaches professional athletes with an enormous natural talent and running history. His plan, also advancing the long run, introduces many other aspects. Different paces and workouts, hills and marathon paced running at the end of long runs. All in all, a very sophisticated training concept with many aspects of running to advance distance as well as ability. In my opinion it is in question if the intermediate runner is able to carry out this plan without burning out. The accumulated stress should be severe.

Pete Pfitzinger's plan presents a good compromise. Long runs are advanced, LT and 5K paces are maintained and marathon pace is employed to get acquainted with the race stress itself. The downside of the approach is that the supporting paces, a concept I value very much, do not play a role and that not all columns of running are introduced. A clear downside to reducing a training plan to accommodate the runner who can handle less than 100 km per week.

Yet, it is possible to learn a lot from these publications as we rarely deal in term of wrong or right but what is called for under certain conditions. If a runner has followed a base cycle for say three months it can be assumed that the endurance base, power and basic speed have been advanced. This can already be called the first period of the marathon cycle. The build phase would take the long run towards or even beyond 2 hours. At this point a runner needs to decide if he will go for the slower and more comfortable approach or the more race specific approach. Like training for a half marathon the marathon provides the option of running closer to endurance pace. For this approach not a lot of speed training is needed. But if actual marathon pace (in the sense of Daniels' tables) is the goal than all the columns of running need to be developed.

In the following we will assume that the endurance base was developed. I.e. a number of base cycles have been gone through for training until easy and endurance pace seize to improve significantly. It is then necessary to adapt the build cycle from what was introduced before. The reason for this is that the advancement of the long run, as present in all aforementioned plans, takes more than a couple of weeks. The time span for race preparation would be all too large to fit two marathons into one year. This in turn seems to be the standard with training plans occupying up to around 20 weeks mostly. In this context, even three base cycles seem excessive since that would be 12 weeks in the example above. This is where the first assumption about training is made: an intermediate runner might not have run many marathons (or any at all). For this type of runner the endurance base if obviously the most significant. The longer the race duration the more endurance and less speed based the race is. Therefore, a more seasoned marathon runner would have to evaluate how much time it takes to reach a plateau in his easy and endurance running paces (compare fig. 11). This procedure, in my opinion, also defines which approach for the marathon race itself a runner should follow. If easy and endurance pace still have not reached the plateau after 8 weeks of training (as in my example) it can be safely assumed that the endurance base is not quite as developed in general. If this runner then follows a training plan with lots of interval running included he might feel like a lot of effort was put into the goal race but it is questionable if that will actually do him any good. The worst case scenario is then that the lactate heavy intervals will have an inverse effect on basic endurance. The final sprint in the race might be great as the result but the 42.1km before that sprint are below the optimum and might even hurt more than needed. Not a good choice in my opinion. Therefore, the first approach for the marathon is to push the endurance base as far as possible. For this type of runner, a marathon might be attempted without any higher pace training beyond LT pace. The training plan for the first ever marathon might than look something like shown in table 26.

Cycle	Base Approach	Seasoned Approach
1	Base 1	Base 1
2	Base 2	Base 2
3	Base 3	Build 1
4	Build 1	Build 2
5	Prep/Race	Prep/Race

Table 26: Training cycle possibilities for the marathon.

The base approach is geared towards the beginner who might want to finish the marathon (maybe even at a great time). I took that approach for a 29K race by making the endurance long run (compare fig. 7) my main workout a couple of weeks before the race. Endurance pace is, as introduced with the half marathon, the goal pace for the marathon as well in this case. Using this approach, the marathon becomes somewhat more predictable as it is leaning on the basic endurance side. Endurance pace for a runner might be around 4:50min/km and marathon pace at around 4:35min/km (according to Daniels' tables). As demonstrated in fig. 7, heart rate can be constant for almost the entire duration of the 24km long run making this a true endurance pace run. The goal for the marathon preparation is then to advance the distance of this steady state heart rate run towards the goal distance of 42.2km, which would imply an endurance run of around 35km two weeks before the race. Counting backwards from the goal race the following schedule results (table 27).

Week	Weekly Goals before marathon race at the end of week 1
1-2	Tapering and maintenance
3-6	Build phase 2 Extension of long run towards 32-35km
7-10	Base 3/Build 1 phase: Extension of long run towards 24km
11-14	Base phase 2 (long run 1.5h)
15-19	Base phase 1 (long run 1.5h)

Table 27: Endurance based schedule for marathon training.

The difficult aspect is to plan for the individual needs of the runner because it depends on what the shortest long run actually amounts to in terms of distance. At an endurance pace of 5:00min/km or faster a runner does not need to worry. 5:00min/km means 18km to 22km for the base phases 1+2, 2:15min for the 24km phase of base 3/ build 1 but already 2:55min for the build phase 2. Anything faster is obviously less time consuming. I would say that a three hour long run is about the maximum duration of the long run as recovery is too time consuming beyond. Subsequently, a much slower runner would need a much longer time to prepare for a marathon, an endeavor I like to discourage and refer to the half marathon until endurance pace has improved somewhat close to 5:00min/km. For the example above, the main question arises as to how to extend the long run from 24km to 32-35km? I would suggest a combined approach from what was mentioned before and taking personal physical limits into account. The standard build cycle (table 12 for a four week cycle) takes a certain long run duration (distance for the marathon plan) and repeats easy long, easy with add-ons and endurance long runs for the given time/distance. Up to 2:15h-2:30h this might work alright and for some athletes even beyond that. For many others, this will simply hurt too much. The runner must then either reduce other workouts of the week in duration and/or intensity or take an alternative approach. The alternative approach I propose is, after completion of week 10

115

(which is a recovery week) to attempt a 35km easy long run. If it works out well the build cycle can be completed by adding more and subsequently running a 35km endurance run which is race pace. If it the easy long run does not work (it really hurts beyond the 24km mark) the runner might want to try and get to 30-32km. The next week is then geared towards an increase in distance as well as adding some sub-LT pace at least, say 32km including a couple of kilometers (maybe as little as two) at sub-LT pace in the middle or the end. The final run of the cycle, three weeks before the goal race, should be at endurance pace and no shorter than 32km, ideally more. Now, many people might argue that the long run should not be carried out at race pace for that long. I tend to agree, yet, race pace was deliberately reduced from marathon pace to endurance pace to make an enjoyable and successful marathon more measurable. At 5:00min/km the result would be a 3:31h marathon time with the theoretical marathon pace being at around 4:45min/km, a 3:20h marathon. Racing below the physical limitations means more manageability. If the final endurance run shows a steady heart rate plateau over the majority even the entire distance of 35km it shows that the body is in steady state over that time and distance. All internal systems of the body are well within comfortable margins and it can be assumed that the final 7km can at least be endured. A lot of gamble is taken out of the whole aspect of training for the first marathon in my opinion.

Obviously, other runs besides the weekly long run are important as well. Yet, the marathon, especially for anybody taking more than 2.5h for it, is defined by long run performance. So what else is necessary? The base cycles improve basic endurance (what your easy and endurance paces actually are), basic power (to have enough muscle mass and strength) and basic speed (to turn over your legs quickly). The build periods are then used to maintain these abilities and to add muscular endurance both at higher paces (sub-LT to LT) while above LT paces are neglected here as basic endurance requires more space in the schedule. The downside to this approach is obvious. If any race faster than at half marathon pace would be attempted during this time, the runner would feel like his legs were too heavy to move adequately. Low heart rate while not being able to endure e.g. 5k pace due to muscle pain is a possible result.

Week	Tue.	Wed.	Thu.	Fri.	Sat.	Sun.
1	Endurance (1h)	Q1 warmup, 5-7x1K@LT pace 1min recovery, cooldown	-	Q2 warmup, sub-LT (20min), cooldown	Easy (1h)	Q3 long easy run (up to 35km)
2	Endurance (1h)	Q1 warmup, 6-8x1K@10K race pace 1-2min recovery, cooldown	-	Q2 warmup, LT (20min), cooldown	Easy to Recovery (up to 1h)	Q3 long easy run with 10-20min sub-LT at the end (up to 35km)
3	Easy (1h)	Q1 warmup, Fartlek with 10min LT HR + 10 min above LT with one hill and different paces, cooldown	-	Q2 warmup, sub-LT (20min), cooldown	Easy to Recovery (up to 1h)	Q3 long endurance (32-35km)
4	Easy to endurance (1h)	-	Easy (1h)	-	Recovery (slow) (45min-1h)	Q3 long easy (24km)

Table 28: Build cycle 2 for endurance based marathon preparation (table 27).

Table 28 shows a possible alteration of the build cycle as the final cycle before the prep/race cycle. This cycle is where the runner can see if his goal is actually attainable. The extension of the long run towards 35km was covered. But as a stand-alone workout it does not say much. The accumulated fatigue of the training weeks is key to improvement the longer the distance gets as well as also tending to the other columns of running. It depends very much on the individual runner if Q1 and Q2 can be carried out and to what extend. When in doubt, cut those workouts short and focus on Q3. Yet, power and speed as well as muscular endurance need at least to be maintained. It is also helpful to add hills into the running course for some of the easy/endurance runs including Q3. The entire focus of the cycle is to find out if all the columns are developed enough to ensure a marathon finish at endurance pace. This is accomplished through the 35K endurance paced run. The final two weeks before the marathon race are devoted to tapering with an increase in intensity. This is identical to the half marathon and endurance paced approach (table 32).

For the endeavor of an endurance paced marathon the anaerobic system may well be underdeveloped as no focus was placed on it at all. At this point a runner might think that this approach to a long endurance race could be a long term solution. He would then repeat base, build and prep/race cycle year after year. But, long term improvement can only happen if all columns of running are equally developed. A runner might be able to push his PB a couple of times with this endurance based approach but the law of diminishing returns will strike down such aspirations quickly. The simple reason is that easy and endurance pace will also seize to improve if 10K and faster paces are entirely avoided. A compromise for the runner who likes to avoid the pain of interval and harder sub-LT or LT running is to add a 5K prep/race cycle after a completed marathon plan. The first one or two weeks after the race should be a recovery week after which the lower volume higher intensity 5K cycle should improve the neglected paces. But then, of course, the runner is not avoiding the dreaded high lactate running after all.

Preparing for a marathon at actual marathon race pace

The difference between any longer race (beyond the half marathon for most runners) carried out at endurance pace or the appropriate race pace (based on Daniels' tables) is that endurance pace is always another word for underperformance on the long distances. Of course, a runner can achieve great race results following the endurance approach. But that is rather dependent on the personal capabilities. If e.g. a world class marathon runner did this he might still achieve a 2:30h result. But he would of course not live up to his potential.

To achieve the individual potential at any given time and training level all the columns of running need to be equally strong with emphasis on what is required by the particular race in question. Of course, the longer the race the more emphasis is placed on basic endurance. But an easy pace of 4:00min/km and faster as often observed with world class athletes is still a 4:00min/km pace. The body has to be able to turn over the legs quickly enough, push off the ground hard enough, have the appropriate length of stride as well as the internal properties such as heart stroke volume and mitochondriatic density, etc. Since, no run solely stresses only one column the runner will improve even if some columns are not specifically addressed during training. But eventually the lack in training balance will show improvement to decrease. This can obviously be caused by approaching the personal maximum but for most runners that is not the case. Especially if the particular runner began his running with half or even marathon races it is often the case that running below the individual potential is the norm.

Similar to the endurance pace approach, many runners still need the base cycles to improve basic endurance, power and speed. Yet, build and prep cycles would look different and would feel much more taxing. Much more caution has to be placed on not to overtrain especially during the build phases. During the endurance approach, mainly the long run was advanced and sub-LT, LT and some 10K pace was inserted to maintain. Now, it becomes an individual venture into what is physically possible. During the build period it is possible that a runner experiences muscle soreness for the entire span of the cycle, not a very pleasant time. Also, some runs will fail or feel not fun at all. The bottom line is that a training plan this close to what is doable needs to be individual. It is of no consequence to copy plans from successful runners simply because that these plans focus on a different person with different needs. However, it is possible to have a certain goal in mind for the upcoming cycle and to scale back from an ambitious plan to avoid crossing the boundary towards overtraining.

The underlying assumption is that whoever tries to run the marathon at actual marathon pace has already run a couple of marathons prior at endurance pace. Thus, the aerobic base is somewhat more developed compared to a fist timer. So we will limit the training to two base cycles. An assumption which can be challenged by following the improvement of easy and endurance paces throughout the cycles once again. Then, the overall plan looks something like in table 29.

Week	Goals before marathon race in week 1
1-2	Tapering and maintenance
3-6	Build phase 2 Extension of long run towards 32-35km and marathon paced runs and 10K and half marathon pace
7-10	Build 1 phase: Extension of long run towards 24km plus extension of sub-LT and LT running plus 3K, 5K,10K pace intervals
11-14	Base phase 2 (long run 1.5h)
15-19	Base phase 1 (long run 1.5h)

Table 29: Marathon pace based schedule for marathon training.

Week	Tue.	Wed.	Thu.	Fri.	Sat.	Sun.
1	Q1 warmup, 5x800m@3K pace 3min recovery, cooldown	Endurance + 2-4 alactic sprints (1h)	-	Endurance (1h)	Easy (1h)	Q3 10K long easy run + 14K@M pace (24km)
2	Q1 warmup, 2-5x 1K@5K race pace 1-2min recovery + 0-3x 800m@3K race pace 3min recovery, cooldown	Endurance+ 2-4 alactic sprints (1h)	-	Q2 warmup, LT (20min), cooldown (1h)	Easy (1h)	Q3 long easy run with 10-20min sub-LT at the end (24km)
3	Q1 warmup, 5-7x 1K@10K race pace 1-2min recovery, cooldown	Easy (1h)	-	Q2 warmup, sub-LT (20-30min), cooldown	Easy (1h)	Q3 long endurance (24km)
4	Easy to endurance (1h)	-	Easy (1h)	-	Recovery (slow) (45min-1h)	Q3 long easy (18km)

Table 30: Example of build 1 cycle for marathon preparation at actual marathon pace.

Table 30 shows a possible build 1 phase for the marathon based approach. Much like for preparing a 10K, the cycle advances the runner towards 10K pace through intervals. At the same time, the long run is extend to 24km. These two aspects of the cycle is set including some alactic sprints for maintenance of basic speed. These sprints can also be done on hills to include some basis power. The Sub-LT to LT runs need to be handled with care. The reason for this is that they introduce a lot of fatigue which might hinder the runner to complete the following long run successfully. Therefore, before the marathon paced run, the sub-LT run is even omitted. Any runner needs to find his individual maximum (sub-)LT distance as the purpose of the cycle is a focus on Q1 and Q3, no necessarily Q2. Q1, though, is a little flexible as the workout depends on the natural abilities of the runner. Someone who has focused on 5K and 10K races can probably lean towards more of the faster intervals while maintaining 5K and 10K pace. Someone with little higher paced training should probably keep the paces even, trying to run a little of all paces.

Table 31 shows an example of a following build 2 cycle which is even more dependent on the runner himself. By now it should be clear that the final cycle before the race should contain lots of race specific paces, in this case namely HM and marathon pace running. Since the now even more stressing Q3 sessions need more recovery Q1 is moved to Wednesday instead of Tuesday.

Week	Tue.	Wed.	Thu.	Fri.	Sat.	Sun.
1	Q1 warmup, 4-6x 1600m@HM pace 1-2min recovery, cooldown	Endurance + 2-4 alactic sprints (1h)	-	Q2 warmup, sub-LT (20-40min), cooldown	Easy (1h)	Q3 long easy + 12-15K@M pace (30km)
2	Easy (1h)	Q1 warmup, alternate 2-3K@HM pace and 1-2K@easy (1-1.5h)	-	Endurance (1h)	Easy (1h)	Q3 long easy (32-35km)
3	Easy + 2-4 alactic sprints (1h)	Q1 warmup, alternate 2-3K@M pace and 1-2K@easy (1-1.5h)	-	Endurance (1-1.5h)	Easy (1h)	Q3 long easy + 15-20K@M pace (30-35km)
4	Easy to endurance (1h)	-	Easy (1h)	-	Recovery (slow) (45min-1h)	Q3 long easy (24km)

Table 31: Example of build 2 cycle for marathon preparation at actual marathon pace.

Also, Q2 is mostly canceled as most runners are just not able to take the stress. Although, if a runner is able to deal with it on a 6 hour per week average training schedule (which is already exceeded by up to 2 hours here), the endurance runs of week 2 and/or 3 can be turned into progression runs. These runs would begin at easy pace

122

and gradually accelerate towards marathon goal pace.

Week	Tue.	Wed.	Thu.	Fri.	Sat.	Sun.
1	Moderate Fartlek with some Tempo at LT and hills (1:00h)	Endurance + 2-4 alactic sprints (1:00h)	-	Easy (1:00h)	recovery (0:45h)	Endurance (1:30h)
2	Easy (0:45-1:00h)	4x90sec@goal race pace 3min recovery at easy pace	3x90sec@goal race pace 3min recovery at easy pace	-	1x90sec@goal race pace 3min recovery at easy pace	Marathon Race @goal race pace

Table 32: Race cycle for marathon goal event.

Table 32 shows the race cycle for both the endurance and marathon pace races. Since the last week of the preceding cycle was already a recovery week week 1 of the race cycle can contain some speed training and possibly some 3K to 10K paced intervals. But for most runners another week of recovery is called for after the high volume running of the two preceding cycles. The final week before the race is then used to reacquaint with race pace.

4.7 Periodization across a season

In the preceding chapters, different training cycles have been introduced. A runner with focus on race results would now take his goal race for the upcoming season (about 6 months in the future) and calculate backwards. So many weeks for race and prep cycle, so many times his personal build and base cycles. The design is dependent on the individual skills and goal races, e.g. if a 1500m runner wants to tackle half marathons he needs more base endurance than before and therefore probably more base than build cycles.

The intermediate runner on the other hand might value fun (at good performance) over performance only. For this type of runner, the majority of all runners, multiple base cycles are a must. Enjoyment of running happens in the aerobic regimen which in turn means that a large aerobic base will prevent any race from starting to slip into anaerobic running all too soon. Also, for this type of runner, it might be too boring to follow a strict plan all by himself. He might e.g. be inclined to run most of his LT runs in a race setting on the weekend. As a result, he might repeat a base cycle three times during the winter months. After that he will design build cycles with a weekly race for LT running and the occasional all out racing while very little actual race preparation in form of prep/race cycles is done. Muscular endurance is build all across spring and summer, maybe a base cycle is placed into the hot summer to then return to the build and racing in the fall. The last races of the season might then be tackled with an actual prep/race cycle. It is obvious that absolute performance in a single (or even multiple) race is not the goal but a high level participation in lots of events. The runner would then balance his running between the maintenance of basic endurance, speed and power while working on muscular endurance, (sub-)LT and some anaerobic running in races or through interval running.

If this more relaxed approach is followed it is important to not completely omit fast pace running. Only if 3K and higher paces are part of the season the return to the base cycle will show further improvement. This is the reason why it makes sense to focus on 5K (maybe in combination with a serious 10K preparation) at the end of a season. The subsequent return to the base cycle in the winter will then lift the runner to the next level. This shift, however, will be absent if the paces between 1500m and 5K are not seriously trained at. A good indication of this phenomenon is that easy run pace improves in the base cycle while LT pace improves more slowly. The gap between them shortens, the build period does not change much there. But during a serious 5K preparation, the gap widens again with easy pace slowing a little but LT and the faster paces improving significantly. The end of this race preparation can be observed when easy pace starts to deteriorate while LT pace seizes to improve.

5 Design of a monthly cycle

Now that the foundation of different directions for training cycles has been established it needs to be discussed as to how a personal training plan is put together. By now, it should be clear that the plans a runner can download off the Internet will only (if at all) work for the final weeks before a race.

In the preceding chapters a lot of assumptions were used for simplicity reasons: how many hours the runner trains during a week (around six), the number of weeks of increasing training load he can bear (four) or that never anything comes up that lets you alter the plan (which always happens). Therefore, just taking the cycles above and using them will probably improve some runners abilities but also probably not as much as possible.

In the following sections, we will take a step by step approach to designing a training plan for any runner. Alternatively, because many runners invest about six hours a week into their running, the cycles presented previously may be altered to result in such a plan.

5.1 Time spend running during training week

The first question when setting up a training plan is: "how much time do I spend training per week?". This question is not too difficult to answer looking at average training history. But for many runners this average number does not say all that much about how many hours they should train for per week. The reason is that for many intermediate runners another fact is missing: consistency. Consistency means how many hours per week a runner is able to train for consistently, i.e. week in week out, without feeling any negative effects (such as injury or burn out) or too little stimulus too improve.

So the first step is to find this appropriate time spend running. In my eyes, this is not a physically restricted number but a choice for most people. Obviously, the more he runs the better a runner is going to get. That much is obvious. Clear is also that the probability of getting injured in the process will also increase exponentially (as many such processes sadly tend to behave). Thus, question becomes how much risk a runner is willing to take for a certain personal best time: choice. The other issue is simply if a runner is willing to take the highest (Olympic athlete kind of) risk the average runner might not want to take. This is especially so since the average runner will probably not make it to the Olympics in lack of natural talent. Therefore, the risk assessment is a choice between a runner's natural abilities and his willingness to achieve it (or as close to it as possible). For the people who want to maximize the outcome the reasoning stops here. For most other people such as myself the number of hours a runner consistently wants or is able to spend training is far lower than all physical constraints.

As the result, a runner might want to take the average number of hours per week he ran in the past and compare to the number of hours per week he wants to invest consistently over a long time (say years). For example, I happened to run around five hours per week over the course of a year during which the actual running time would fluctuate between three and six hours weekly. On the other hand, the number of hours I felt were sensible to devote to running came out to be about six, which is four days of running one hour each plus the Sunday long run of around two hours. My first step was then to bring the two numbers together, that is to increase my weekly running to six hours consistently which I did step by step using the method I introduced in table 5. From a retrospective it would probably have been much wiser to train with less tempo training in the training cycles to up my chosen weekly load. The resulting cycle might look like something displayed in table 33.

Step	Tue.	Wed.	Fri.	Sat.	Sun.
1 (3.75h)	10K LT (1.25h)	-	10K LT (1.25h)	-	1.25h slow
2 (4h)	10K LT (1.25h)	-	10K LT (1.25h)	-	1.5h slow
3 (4.5h)	8K LT (1h)	1h slow	8K LT (1h)		1.5h slow
4 (5h)	Hill LT runs + Endurance run (1h)	1h slow	8K LT (1h)		2h slow
5 (5.5h-6h)	Hill LT runs + Endurance run (1h)	1h slow + 2-4 8sec sprints	8K LT (1h)	30min to 1h slow	2h slow

Table 33: Stepwise approach to reach personal running goal in hours. Monday, some core strength workout can be done and Thursday is rest day.

The table is derived from the base cycle and will help improve the endurance base. It begins with lots of LT running because that is what many people subconsciously train without plan or other training guide. Any additional step, the length of the newly introduced workout (or the number of repetitions) should be started relatively on the safe side, not doing as much as described in the table but slowly easing into it. So week by week a little more is done and the body has the time to adjust to the load. Also, a transformation from LT running towards more base cycle-like running is introduced. It will take probably about one year of training for the tendons to adjust to the new demands and get through all the steps. During this time, injuries are probable because all the slowly changing systems (bones, tendons, ligaments) will not hurt at first and then suddenly become inflamed. It is thus a good idea to give the body some time to ease into each step. A runner might be able to do it much faster if prior training (maybe in a different sport) has prepared him for the workload. But make no mistake, increasing the weekly duration of running is the most common cause for injuries. Comparing this to my own example mentioned earlier, I would have begun around step 3 to 4 and would have gotten used to every step until six weekly hours of training are the standard implying a total time of change to be less than a year.

During the time of load adjustment it is also not advised to train by a complex plan that is supposed to increase intensity over say a monthly cycle. Too often, these combined stresses of high paced running, exercises a runner is not used to and the increased hours of training pushes him over the edge and into long term injury. Best to increase load first (in base cycle training) and then go through a more complex cycle with a maximum weekly running time just a little above the maximum a runner is used to through the step-wise approach.

5.2 The connection between training time and number of sessions per week

Now that a runner has decided how many hours a week he wants to train for he must distribute the workouts over the course of a training week. While theoretically the imagination is not limited to seven day cycles most runners end up using the week as a guideline. This is because for most runners the training plan is not optimized to the extreme where the alternation of stress to the body and the subsequent recovery/adaption is analyzed for the individual needs. In theory, if (over a period of time) every run and all recovery time would be analyzed for optimal recovery time and best stress adaption scenarios you might come up with cycles lasting 10 days or more.

Since we are discussing the intermediate runner trying to improve ample recovery time is available. Again, in theory, as the informed reader might say, still many hobby runners get injured. The reason is that even though the hobby of running is the topic many athlete's training regimes are not very far away from what professional runners do. It only depends on two aspects: running time compared to number of high intensity runs per week. These in turn depend on the goal distance. If we assume that professional runners do the optimum needed to maximize their performance in any given situation we are able to derive how far a hobby runner fares compared with this maximum. Take e.g. German professional runner Arne Gabius (www.arnegabius.de). Arne is a career runner who started out with shorter distance running ultimately setting out to breaking the German marathon record. He published some of his training schedule on his website. This publication shows e.g. that during any given training week he rarely (except tapering periods) runs less than a hundred kilometers a week with peak training weeks at well over 200km. To a hobby runner these are impressive numbers. But looking a little closer reveals that he also rarely runs slower than a 3:50min/km pace which seems to constitute Arne's slow run. Since we know his personal best in the 10K was 27min44sec at the time on the track (2:46min/km) this slow running pace (of about 1min/km slower) makes sense as easy pace. Roughly the same relationship holds true in the example of table 4. Therefore, while being enormously quick on his feet every day a typical training week of 200km might be a little shy of 13 hours for Arne. And this is having the marathon in mind where long slow running is one of the main training stresses. Training for a 5K track PB requires a lot more short and fast running during certain training periods which also reduces running hours per week for a pro.

Thus, if a hobby runner clocks 10 hours per week plus job and family requirements we are already talking about a semi professional training regime even though much less distance might be covered. If on top of that the 5K PB training plan is followed the runner might even be on the professional level without realizing it. Also, it took Arne Gabius, as well as every other Olympic type athlete, 20 or more years to slowly approach this peak level. All these aspects considered, injuries are much more likely than hobby runners believe, too many training hours with too many stressful training sessions are a sure recipe for a severe and lasting injury.

So how shall we approach training plan setup towards the optimum? The first step is, as explained earlier, to run a certain number of hours per week and to approach this number consistently and carefully over an extended period of time. This might be done as shown in table 33. The key element is that so-called quality runs are distributed over the week. Quality (Q) runs are all runs not falling inside the easy or endurance run column including the long run. It seems plausible at first glance that faster paced running stresses the body out more than slower paced runs. But why is this the case? The answer is not at all simple but can be simplified for the sake of the argument. Every training run stresses out all the columns of running in a different way. The body has mechanisms to trigger adaption to higher levels of ability (supercompensation) which work through inflammation mechanisms. A harsh LT run type workout might result in some muscle tears, some tendon stress and an overall stress on the respiratory system including the heart. The body reacts with mild inflammation in all those corners of the runner's body. On the following rest day(s) inflammation levels subside, damage is repaired. If a runner adds the next quality run the following day after the first run inflammation levels would increase and fatigue might even prevent a good performance. The adaption process might be derailed. Overtraining syndrome is (among other things) just that: a body-wide inflammatory reaction being out of control. Total rest is needed for an extended period of time. The principle of hard training days being followed by easy (or rest) days which in turn are followed by another hard training day and so on is key to balancing an effective training.

Therefore, the number of runs and the number of quality (Q) runs per week need to be chosen carefully. Most people can take two to three quality sessions a week. This approach is the foundation of the progression in table 33. After defining the number of Q sessions a week they need to be spaced. Three Q runs, the number I recommend as a starting point can be distributed in different ways. But since more runners want to do their long run (Q3) on Sunday the next Q sessions make either Tuesday/Friday or Tuesday/Thursday sensible options. Either way, a runner will always have one vs. two rest/easy days between Q days. Also, the type of Q days need to be chosen. I like to separate two tempo/strength/speed related Q running days on Tuesday and Friday and one distance related Q run on Sunday. What needs to be understood is that even though each Q session might be taxing the column that is not in focus will also not be trained, it might even be in recovery mode. Let's assume a runner does a hill tempo run on Tuesday training force and some LT. An LT run following on Friday emphasizes the combination of all columns without overstressing any of them while a long easy run on the Sunday afterward might even aid to recovery. That long run will help improve endurance which at least needs to be maintained. As a result, the Q runs need a certain amount of time and a certain day in a training week. This leaves the rest of the training hours to be scheduled around them.

A good rule of thumb is that any single run should at least have 20min of duration as the absolute minimum recovery run. A good minimum time for an easy run is around 30min. Also, at least one day a week should be kept off running entirely, for most runners it will be two days. Up until six to eight hours of training per week two off days are the norm. This leaves most runs to be one to 1.5 hours each with the long run between 1.5 and 2.5 hours time. Again, a good rule of thumb is to increase training length with overall duration per week and to spread time evenly across the week. It is important to note that with increasing duration per week no additional Q sessions are added but more of easy/endurance running. The reason for this is that the endurance column is very hard to develop. It takes lots of time to improve it while high tempo sessions even diminish that column. Thus, lucky for us, enjoyable easy and endurance running become more emphasized the more an athlete runs. Ultimately, 80% of running ends up in the easy/endurance corner as pointed out by Matt Fitzgerald in "80/20 running". While I recommend the book for many reasons I do not support the argument that the relationship between easy/endurance running and higher tempo running (80/20) holds true for all runners. I merely think that a pro runner will arrive somewhere close to this ratio while running very low volume (e.g. 3h per week as a beginner) will lean towards LT pace and maybe short and harder intervals.

For the novice runner, Q sessions are what they often subconsciously start with (emphasizing LT running mostly). The resulting speed distribution over a week improves the beginners abilities simply because of the fact that any faster type of running done consistently will improve the runner's PB at that point. This is the environment where e.g. HIIT (High intensity interval training) was tested. Athletes with little training background were tested for improvement of speed by comparing low intensity exercise with a HIIT regime. It was found that HIIT helped significantly better with improvement. The reason is simple: intensity means lots of stress to the body which is translated into supercompensation during the 4-5 rest days for the novice runner. For a couple of weeks, this relationship will hold true, the runner will improve quickly. But the law of diminishing returns will soon kick in. Any additional training week will result in a smaller additional improvement until the runner gets stuck. So what then? More HIIT intervals? More HIIT sessions? The answer is a simple NO as all columns of training need to be developed as a runner progresses. For the beginner, more intensity with 3-5 rest days is plausible. But e.g. for six hours of running per week, HIIT has absolutely no place in a training plan except on maybe a Q day. But then, it is just a regular interval session.

The bottom line is that the more running an athlete adds to his schedule the more easy/endurance running he will likely need while keeping the faster/harder sessions constant or slightly increasing them (e.g. 8x1K instead of 6x1K intervals). This is one of the reasons how mostly the better runner enjoys running more as simply more and more of his running is in the most enjoyable regime (a strong incentive to improve!).

But where is the maximum? The answer is also a guideline derived from professional athlete's plans (compare table 34). While the long run always stands out at least a little no other session increases past the 1.5h mark because that would be another long run. So let's assume a runner adds more and more hours to his running with a two hour long run on Sunday and two 1.5h Q sessions (=5h per week). At that point three more days would be filled with an hour easy/endurance running resulting in a total of eight hours with one day off. Now the seventh day could be filled with an easy run, nine hours are the maximum for this runner. For longer long runs the entire schedule might tend towards more weekly duration implying distances beyond the marathon. Returning to the example (of a 10K to half marathon runner), adding more time than the mentioned eight hours per week means adding a second run at first on some and then step by step on most if not on all days. At that point, the runner's life alternates between running and resting and little else, a high end plan reserved for professionals and wannabes.

	Mo.	Tue.	Wed.	Thu.	Fri.	Sat.	Sun.
4h	-	Q1 1.25h	-	-	Q2 1.25h	-	Q3 1.5h
5h	-	Q1 1h	Easy 1h	-	Q2 1h	-	Q3 2h
6h	-	Q1 1h	Easy 1h	-	Q2 1h	Easy 1h	Q3 2h
7h	-	Q1 1.5h	Easy 1h	-	Q2 1.5h	Easy 1h	Q3 2h
8h	-	Q1 1.5h	Easy 1h	Easy 1h	Q2 1.5h	Easy 1h	Q3 2h
9h	Easy 1h	Q1 1.5h	Easy 1h	Easy 1h	Q2 1.5h	Easy 1h	Q3 2h
10h	Easy 1h	Q1 1.5h	Easy 1h Easy 1h	Easy 1h	Q2 1.5h	Easy 1h	Q3 2h
11h	Easy 1h	Q1 1.5h	Easy 1h Easy 1h	Easy 1h	Easy 0.5h Q2 1.5h	Easy 1h	Q3 2.5h
12h	Easy 1h	Q1 1.5h	Easy 1h Easy 1h	Easy 1.5h	Easy 1h Q2 1.5h	Easy 1h	Q3 2.5h

Table 34: Hours of training vs. weekly training distribution (easy can also be an endurance run).

Table 34 shows one possible way of progressing and more importantly distributing training hours over the course of a week. The weeks beyond 9h each would be more and more adjusted to the individual needs of the runner. This is because the load approaches more and more the absolute maximum any given runner is able to take on. Therefore, the weekly training load between professional runners varies widely as it should for intermediate runners who attempt these high loads.

The described systematic to distributing the training runs started with the premise of the long run on a Sunday. Of course any other could be a starting point as well. For somebody e.g. working in the restaurant industry this may very well be the Monday. Then the whole distribution shifts a day forward.

5.3 Designing the monthly training cycle

On the foundation of the weekly training cycle the monthly cycle will now be designed. The main question, as mentioned before, is how many weeks of increased load and/or intensity can a runner endure before a recovery week will help with supercompensation. My approach was simple: I started out with a three week plan of increased duration with the fourth week being the recovery week of around 75% load and reduced number of Q sessions. If a runner can take only two weeks before needing recovery a similar procedure can be followed. Every Q session is somewhat advancing the similar preceding one (a week before), increasing the number of intervals, the duration of LT and long runs. This results in "ideal" cycles for base, build and prep/race phases ("ideal" because the plan needs to be adjusted as you go which will be covered below).

The approach is begun with a certain number of hours of training per week a runner becomes accustomed to over a relatively long time. With periodic monthly cycles, workouts very specific to certain columns of running are now added. These workouts require more recovery time than the uniform repetitive training the runner is used to. As a result, weekly hours are distributed around the third week of the monthly cycle, the week of peak load. The first time peak load is still lower or equal than the usual load. Every time the cycle is repeated (three times in the example) the maximum load in week three increases until it surpasses the usual load. At that point a possible limit for the cycle may be reached.

Week	Month 1	Month 2	Month 3
1	5h	5.5h	6h
2	5.5h	6h	6.5h
3	6h	6.5h	7h
4	3.5h	4h	4.5h

Table 35: Monthly cycle for an example of 6 hours weekly usual load.

Table 35 shows a possible progression for a runner adjusted to 6 hours of weekly training. The new workouts as well as the increasing load over the weeks make it necessary to begin a little below the 6 hour mark. But it will become clear very soon how much load is too much. Thus, it will also become clear if the proposed increase can actually be executed in practice. The bottom line is that some increase should happen and that week three of the cycle should make the runner feel quite exhausted. My own experience pretty much always resulted in Q1 (first quality run of the week) during the recovery week to be going quite well. But the next days felt like I could not complete an intense workout at all which left me feeling relieved I only had to do easy runs.

Week	Month 1	Month 2	Month 3
1	5h	5.5h	6h
2	5.5h	6h	6h
3	6h	6h	6h
4	3.5h	4h	4.5h

Table 36: Example time increase for a possible maximum of six hours training per week.

Table 36 shows an example where the maximum training time of six hours per week can not be exceeded. This is usually the case when fatigue becomes too large to further advance the training load which is typical for the build cycle. Following the philosophy of more is better but too much is worse (as it leads to injury) the cycle ends with all three weeks being carried out to the possible maximum of six hours in the example. Since fatigue is accumulated during the cycle the training stress is actually higher during the final 6 hours week than during the first one. The recovery week might be modulated a little bit and it might take a cycle or two (in this case) to find out the maximum training load. It is the intensity and the changing workouts that make up so much additional stress that the maximum can not be exceeded. Still, the runner will take away a gain as intensity at that load is improved but not the load itself.

A good measure to go by in terms of how many hours of training a runner can take is the number of intense quality runs per week. A build phase consisting of two to three high paced runs (such as LT intervals, long endurance runs, etc.) per week might be very challenging. Therefore, to go as high as the weekly duration a runner is used to (six hours in our example) might be the maximum. The runner might be used to the weekly duration, he might even be used to all the workouts. But the combination of high impact fast running and the increased duration will set an individual limit. In some case, the introduction of a single workout that emphasizes a running column normally not trained might result in severe soreness during the entire cycle. Overall, during a base cycle progression it is much easier to increase the weekly load as the Q sessions are less challenging.

It is important to note that two runners may have different maximums but that does not mean the runner who can take more will also have a better race performance (unless the race is about how much running you can do in a week). Remember it is about triggering improvements with the least possible amount of training. Following this philosophy, between two runners of similar race performance, the one with less training load per week has possibly the higher potential. If the level of fatigue is so high that the recovery week is not enough to start a fresh new cycle too much work was done before. This is especially true if the runner slips into overtraining or injury which both require very long recovery periods. Thus, the underlying concept of these training cycles is the accumulation of fatigue.

At this point the number of hours per week across a cycle are defined along with when Q workouts take place. Now, the question remains which Q workouts to execute. The answer to this question is defined by the phase a runner trains in (base, build, etc.) and the individual strengths and weaknesses he wishes to improve upon.

Phase	Columns of Training and emphasis

Base	• Endurance
	   ○ Easy and endurance runs
	   ○ Increasing duration and pace of long runs
	   ○ Muscular endurance through sub-LT to LT progression
	• Power
	   ○ Hill LT runs
	   ○ Weights
	• Speed
	   ○ Alactic sprints
	   ○ Short intervals with long recovery

Build	• Endurance
	   ○ LT runs,
	   ○ Endurance runs,
	   ○ (Maintain basic endurance, easy runs)
	• Power
	   ○ (Maintain through hilly courses)
	• Speed
	   ○ Introduce some lactic intervals
	   ○ Above LT finish of LT runs
	   ○ (Maintain alactic speed through sprints)

Peak/Race	• Endurance
	   ○ (LT, anaerobic endurance, maintain basic endurance)
	• Power (no focus)
	• Speed
	   ○ Lactic intervals,
	   ○ Test races at higher speed
	   ○ (no alactic intervals)

Table 37: Columns of training emphasized during different training

phases.

Table 37 shows the general progression of training phases and the changing columns to be improved. It is quite plausible that the individual natural skills of a runner influence the emphasis of each phase. A trained 400m runner might have highly developed speed and power columns but might also lack endurance skills if he begins training for 5K races (the longer the race the more pronounced this deficit becomes). For this runner, the base phase might maintain power and speed and place a heavy load on endurance running of different paces and durations. For a runner who finishes multiple marathons per year on the other hand without any speed training in his plan, power and speed columns might be pronounced. These extreme examples are easy to figure out. For the rest of the runners it might be just that certain workouts were never done before (hill LT runs, LT running, alactic sprints or long endurance runs are likely candidates). For these runners focusing on columns never trained before is always a good idea.

So the next step is which columns to focus on even though the general direction is defined by the kind of cycle. Taking into account the distribution of Q- and the total number of sessions per week the training plan leaves a few but important choices.

	Mo.	Tue.	Wed.	Thu.	Fri.	Sat.	Sun.
6h Base	-	Q1 1h P, S, (E)	Easy 1h E, (S)	-	Q2 1h LT, (E)	Easy 1h (E)	Q3 2h E, (LT)
6h Build	-	Q1 1h LT, S, (E), (AE)	Easy 1h E, (S)	-	Q2 1h LT, S, (E), (AE)	Easy 1h E	Q3 2h E, (LT), (P)
6h Prep/ Race	-	Q1 ? AE, S, LT	Easy ? E	-	Q2 ? LT, AE, (E)	Easy ? E	Q3 ? E, LT, AE

Table 38: Skills per training cycle for the example of 6h and 5

sessions of training per week. E=Endurance Column, LT=Lactate Threshold, AE=Anaerobic endurance, P=Power Column, S=Speed Column,

Table 38 shows the remaining choices for a given training cycle with set number of training hours and workouts per week. The letters in brackets point to the maintenance of skills through add-ons such as a 3K LT run in the middle of a long run. Also, the question marks in the prep/race cycle allude to the fact that for different goal races the focus will be placed on different skills and varying workout length. Obviously, the distribution of skills also looks a bit different for various number of runs per week. But I do believe that the quality sessions should emphasize the columns of running in a way that is challenging to the runner. Easy runs, in my opinion, can not be Q sessions, they help with recovery and basic endurance and no more. Table 38 also shows that it is hard to progress all the running skills in a cycle. Combination workouts training more than one skill will be necessary. This leads to the development of Fartlek and other types of workouts.

The base phase is the easiest because few skills are focused on. Advancing length and intensity of easy and endurance runs are key to this cycle as well as gaining power through hill runs and basic speed through alactic sprints and short intervals. It is relatively basic to design a plan with 5 sessions per week but already a compromise has to be made. Say, the three Q sessions are devoted to hill LT (Q1), LT (Q2) and the long run (Q3) and two easy/endurance runs. The runner chose hill LT runs (Q1) over basic speed development maybe because his speed base is quite developed already. In this case he would have to maintain basic speed by adding e.g. alactic sprints to easy/endurance runs, LT runs or long runs. In our example, the Tuesday/Wednesday combination is ideal to add speed to the Wednesday run after doing a Tuesday power session. The reason for this is the rest day before and after. I would not advise to add anything to the Saturday workout as it is needed for recovery. But the compromise remains, more workouts would mean more options to devote single workouts to a certain skill. But if a runner wishes to train at the most optimum level he might end up with six days a week of two a day training sessions. This is obviously not suitable for most runners out there.

Generally, the more runs an athlete does per week the more freedom exists to work on specific skills in a single session. A professional runner training e.g. 13 hours on multi-day sessions on all seven days per week is very flexible and can adjust to the recovery requirements of individual running sessions. This is really the reason why the training week is designed the way we see it here. A long endurance run of two hours might take 7 days or more to repeat fully recovered. But it is possible to do LT intervals just two days afterwards and an LT run three days after that. The better a runner understands how much recovery a certain running session implies for himself the better a training plan can be designed. For example, I found that I can run 5-7x1K@10K pace intervals just two days after an endurance long run but it takes me five days to be able to run a 30min LT run. This has to some extend to do with the different systems of the body that are especially challenged during a certain run. A long endurance run is hard on the heart/lung system leading to an elevated resting heart rate but lots of stress is placed on the muscles and tendons. LT intervals, speed interval, alactic intervals present a strong challenge on the heart/lungs as well but are less taxing for muscles and tendons. The heart/lung system needs more recovery during the session resulting in elevated heart rates even during recovery between intervals while the muscles feel better after a short while. Therefore, all training plans make use of the fact that the different skills can be trained even if other skills are already in need of recovery.

Base cycles are often somewhat independent of the race a runner trains for as the season highlight. Basic endurance is needed for all race distances. The build cycle already presents a difference for varying race distances as the long run will be significantly more important the longer the race distance. For the marathon, the long run needs to be advanced during many months and is by definition the most important run. 5K runners might cut the long run down to a 1.5 hour maximum with speed add-ons every week (compare table 19). During the prep/race cycle a very race specific training plan is carried out which ideally approaches the race requirement from both sides (fast/short; slow/long). The training plans you find on the Internet often times only represent prep/race cycles which is the very reason why many hobby runners never reach their potential as base and build periods are simply omitted altogether. Also, many hobby runners want to compete in many different events because they are fun and not necessarily get into peak shape for just one or two events in a given year. For those athletes, base and build phases are especially important as race specific fitness only lasts a couple of weeks so those runners might as well stay in the build phase most of the season and carry out short race preparation weeks or even run a race as a workout session. The later is done by many professional runners as a means to make money. Minor 10K road races are used as LT runs which might mean a quick 31 minutes for an Olympic level runner.

5.4 How to put it all together?

In the previous sections it was introduced how to design weekly and monthly training cycles. It is now obvious that very different approaches can be taken towards the individual season setup.

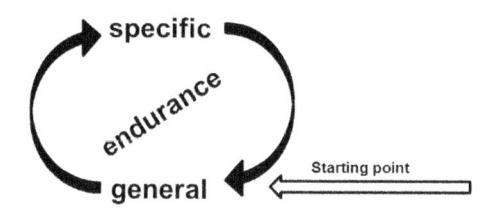

Fig 14: Progression cycle from general to race specific endurance.

The general approach is introduced in fig. 14, the starting point is always the emphasis on general endurance which is always established through one to several base cycles. Once that base is established an athlete can progress to more specific cycles such as the build cycle before establishing race specific fitness. Column by column beginning with base endurance all the columns are progressed while the preceding ones are maintained along the way. At the end of that cycle, after the last race, peak fitness can no longer be maintained, an athlete has to start at the beginning. Luckily, since all columns have been improved and maintained the new base cycle will help shift performance to all new levels. Therefore, cycle after season cycle performance will improve. Also, more stimulus in form of more training load and intensity is needed along the way. The adaption of heart rate based training towards faster paces are a natural progression while interval paces have to be adjusted along the way. Still, at step by step in an athlete's running career the seasonal improvements will slow until they come to a halt altogether.

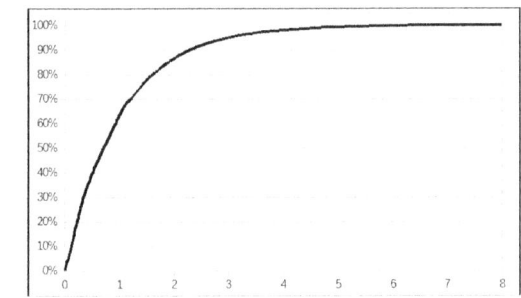

Fig 15: Example for athlete's improvement curve over the years.

Fig. 15 shows the progression of a sample athlete over the years. In this case, the athlete reaches around 60% of his potential after the first year of training and levels off quickly afterwards, not a very fortunate individual. Even though most athletes should approach their potential after many years of training the intermediate runner trains under less than ideal conditions and has probably begun training in his adulthood. Thus, the slope of the displayed curve needs to be found out for every individual which is rather straight forward. The progression of a personal best time in a specific race can be plotted for each year of training. This way the personal position on the progression curve and maybe even its slope can be estimated.

5.4.1 Training goals

As described in the majority of training books, the athlete is supposed to define a so-called "A-race", the peak race of the season then calculate backwards towards the starting point of the training plan. This race-focused cycle is a reasonable approach for a competitive runner whose advances in the world of running are defined by race performance in often times a single race. For these athletes the classic base, build and race cycle approach is the path to success.

For many intermediate runners such a peak race does not exist. They much rather look for races that e.g. fit their schedule, are on the scenic track or other reasons. For these athletes the base cycle is often times followed by a combination of build and race cycle as ultimate race specific fitness is stretched out over a longer period of time. Also, the ultimate peak fitness for a single season highlight is probably not reached but as other factors are more important to the runner this is also not critical.

Regardless which approach a runner takes it is practical to define the beginning of a yearly cycle in the winter where races are race and the weather tends to be colder.

5.4.2 Improving the base

At the beginning of a new season, actually right after the last race of the last season ends, the new base cycle is begun. Contrary to popular belief, no off-season without any endurance sport exists. This is mainly due to the fact that basic endurance is built over years of consistent training which is severely impaired by say a month of downtime at the end of the running year. Even if an ultra race is done at the end of a running year which needs a longer recovery period a runner can still cross train during this time, e.g. ride a bike. Thus, depending on the need for recovery, one or even several weeks of slow running or cross training often mark the beginning of a yearly cycle. The goal is to reduce muscle strain and start the cycle in a fully recovered state. Depending on the state of fatigue this recovery period might last up to a couple of weeks but mostly one or two weeks will do. The runner should feel recovered and motivated to get into the new season.

Now the new base cycle should be designed. If a large variety of different race types will be attempted in the new season I would recommend two to three base cycles as the foundation of the season. The rule of thumb is here that the shorter (and faster) the season races will be the base endurance can be reduced. But for most intermediate runners two to three cycles is a good number. Second, it should be clear from the preceding season what strengths and weaknesses in terms of running columns were. Generally, no single column should be neglected during the base phase, which I find the most important phase, but adjustments can always be made. The analysis of race effort, heart rate and feel during the latest races tell a lot about where adjustments need to be made.

Race observation	Needed adjustment
Heart rate slips into anaerobic regime in first half of 10K or faster race	• Base phase needs extension (adding another cycle) • Strength column emphasis
Prep/race cycle intervals could not be run at faster paces. Races run at slower pace and heart rate, goal missed	• alactic sprints emphasized in base period and maintained throughout entire season • emphasis on 30sec sprints with more repetitions
Hills and race surges could not be followed and were the reason for not keeping up in race	• more emphasis on Fartleks • Hilly courses for easy runs with pace increases into endurance pace or faster during easy runs
Race distance could not be sustained. Heavy muscular fatigue after 2/3 of race distance maybe even at lower heart rates as expected	• muscular endurance should be pronounced with longer LT and sub-LT runs (a little slower but longer) • strength column with longer hill portions
Running economy falls apart during later part of race	• 30sec sprints seem more important to maintain than alactic sprints throughout season • core stability exercises should be focused on

Table 39: Adjustment for base cycles design specific to athlete.

Table 39 shows some typical issues during the preceding race season. It is important to mention that these adjustments should induce slight changes into a base phase training plan. Let's assume that hills and surges presented a problem during the race season while performance during flat surface races was great. This means that the preceding race preparation was sufficient with a small problem. If an athlete now focuses on hills and surges only his race performance will likely not improve due to lack in other areas. Thus, whatever the runner was doing was right with the exception that one ability was not trained. It is therefore easy to introduce hilly courses into easy and endurance runs and add surges of a minute or two into e.g. sub-LT pace into these runs as well. Key would be to teach the body that change in pace is nothing unusual. For the outsider unfamiliar with this runner the changes might not even be visible. Carried out over the course of an entire season this will likely do the trick.

As a result, after understanding how many hours per week during set number of runs an athlete can do on a regular basis and knowing the focus aspects of the base cycle each base cycle can be designed. Key is to vary the cycles in terms of the individual workouts to make sure the body does not get used to the specific training regimen. All in all, the focus should be on extending overall running time per week. Q1 is devoted to the cycle specific column (strength and/or basic speed), Q2 is focused on the maintenance of muscular endurance (sub-LT and LT runs) and Q3 is the long run (easy, endurance with add-ons for sub-LT). Every other run is simply an easy or an endurance run as running at the upper level of the basic endurance window will have the largest effect on advancement of the endurance column.

Key to designing a reasonable training plan is to define workouts at or a bit above the runner's current abilities. If an effect is reached with less training that is always good but preparing a plan that is too easy will not help much. Therefore a runner must listen to his body and cut workouts short if fatigue is too high. Sometimes, although unlikely in a base cycle, a recovery week has to be scheduled to get back into the rhythm of training hard.

For the intermediate runner, as mentioned before, the base cycle should be seen as the most important phase of the season. Extra work here, one more hill LT repeat, one additional sprint will later pay out very well while progression of easy and endurance paces should be closely monitored. If theses paces level out it is time to progress to the build phase. This is also the reason why it does not make sense to keep adding more and more base cycles. Easy and endurance pace would no longer improve (much), the gap between easy and LT pace might stay below 45 sec/km which is a good indication to begin work on the faster sub-LT and LT paces.

5.4.3 Improving lactate threshold level

Now that the base was build through several base cycles the runner is presented with a situation that is less than ideal for racing especially in faster races. Easy and endurance pace have improved quite a bit while LT pace has only slight increased. What is worse, LT runs might feel quite strange now: the heart rate rarely increases beyond LT level or does not even reach it any more. Yet, legs feel tired and it seems that muscular endurance is limiting performance at faster paces. Looking back at what the training goal for the preceding months was this is only a logical consequence. The body is now used to run more efficiently at paces up to endurance pace. New muscular structures are build through hill tempo running and different forms of short sprints. Running quite slowly and running very fast has improved. Performance at all the race distances between will now suffer or at least not improve. This situation also marks the reason why a longer race beyond the half marathon run at endurance pace makes sense in this phase of the yearly cycle. It can easily be sustained without impairing the result of later races too much.

For the runner who wishes to improve the personal bests at races between 800m and the half marathon, especially for 5K and 10K races, the time has come to push LT pace higher and improve muscular endurance towards goal race distance. After all, what is improved sprinting ability good for if this improved speed does not translate to faster race times at all distances? Thus, the build phase starts with an unfamiliar feeling: train what you feel like you are currently bad at. Table 38 shows this change in training goal between base and build cycle. Q1 is now devoted to LT up to 10K pace intervals and Fartleks. Q2 are standard sub-LT to LT runs which, depending on the training goal, will follow either the guideline of increasing distance at set pace or increasing pace at set distance over the course of the cycle. If unsure, the runner can always switch between these approaches from one build cycle to the next and monitor improvement of LT pace as well as the distance for which LT pace can be sustained. If a runner enters the build cycle with very low muscular endurance it would be wise to begin with increasing distance at LT pace weekly since sub-LT running should not be a problem at this point.

From the base cycle, weekly training hours and number of sessions per week will already be known. This knowledge can directly be translated to the build cycle as with the increased training intensity of the build cycle the weekly training duration can hardly be increase any more. Yet, keeping duration per week constant while increasing overall intensity will lead to more distance run weekly. The build cycle shows rather directly how much a runner can take in terms of training volume at intensity. A middle ground needs to be found between maintaining the achievements of the base cycles while advancing intensity. Care should be taken not to run LT runs at a pace that drives the heart rate above LT HR. This would diminish basic endurance and prevent the runner from further improvement. This is the reason why Q1 will contain some intervals slightly above LT pace with the ability of the body to metabolize lactic acid while LT runs will be kept below the threshold. This combination will shift LT pace over time. Running the weekly long run at the maximum duration achieved during the base phase might not be possible because emphasis is clearly on a good performance during the Q1 and Q2. Q3 is strictly for maintenance purposes while adding on LT to the long run will help as well. The trade off happens most likely between Q2 and Q3 as either the long run or LT run distance can be increased over the cycle, likely not both.

The method above (advancing LT distance over the long run) would have the purpose of preparing for races below the half marathon. The advanced LT pace and muscular endurance can be used for the subsequent prep/race cycle for peak performance. Also, the build phase is very well suited for the more fun oriented runner. Depending on the current endurance pace Q3 can be substituted occasionally for a half marathon race run between endurance and sub-LT pace. Q2 is then reduced in length, if more than 30min were scheduled and additional LT running is done during the final 5K of the half marathon race if possible. Ideally, the following week would be a recovery week for obvious reasons but does not necessarily have to be if the runner can sustain the load. The other end of the spectrum would be 10K races substituting Q2 or Q3 which are run at LT pace.

These races are an excellent way to increase muscular endurance and see how long LT pace follows LT HR as any runner will slow at LT HR after a while. 5K races at LT can always substitute for Q2, for Q3 an extended warm up could precede such a race and should be followed by a long cool down to constitute a long run. However, shorter races than a 5K do not make much sense as time at LT would be too short and the pace of the other runners likely too high. Therefore, build cycles are highly flexible in terms of scenic or fun races. The runner simply has to keep in mind not to exceed LT HR.

Race/base observation	Needed adjustment
Muscular endurance is lacking	• increase time at LT pace step by step towards 40min • when maximum is reached, pace can be varied to consider recovery requirements • Alternatively, long sub-LT runs can be scheduled (e.g. 9-15K between endurance and LT pace)
Race scenario was difficult in past season (e.g. getting used to race excitement)	• Use multiple races as training sessions as LT run or long run • include surges and hills into KT and easy running
Prep/race showed inability to perform intervals at given 1.5K and/or 3K paces	• maintain alactic sprints throughout the cycle • add few (2-3) 1.5K and 3K intervals to LT intervals with lots of recovery

Table 40: Adjustment for build cycles design specific to athlete.

Table 40 summarizes some possible adjustments to be made to the build cycle. For the most part, the build cycles are much less influenced by the previous race season as the base cycle is. Its main purpose is to advance LT pace and improve muscular endurance which is dictated by the base cycle itself.

Mostly, two build cycles are needed to do the trick. Over the weeks, it will feel more familiar to run longer at LT pace while that pace should improve. At some point, enough muscular endurance is built to take on some more serious race preparation. For an intermediate runner attempting longer races such as the marathon or beyond tougher races might already be on the schedule during the late build cycle. This is due to the reason that those races are often extended endurance runs. The races can be prepared for without diverting from the build cycle but by extending Q3 and keeping LT running at Q2 somewhat shorter (e.g. 20-30min). However, if done over several seasons, any runner will experience a leveling off of personal performance as the anaerobic system is completely neglected during base and build cycles. Even though this system is hardly needed for long races exceeding half marathons it is necessary to stress the muscles to a point only possible by running up higher levels of lactic acid. Professional runners advancing from 5K or 10K racing towards the marathon sometimes only maintaining their speed by injecting 1.5K or 3K intervals into the training plan. But these runners want to maintain their shorter distance speed, not improve it. For the intermediate runner on the other hand improvement is key.

5.4.4 The cycle of improvement

By now it should be clear that single workouts or even single cycles (such as goal race training plans downloaded off the internet) have little consequence to the longer term improvement of any runner. The very same interval session, or even a whole progression of runs towards a goal, would trigger different adaptations inside the body depending on previous training. A perfect prep/race cycle would still only push an athlete into anaerobic adaption without the proper base and build cycles. All training columns need to advance if the personal best times in all races shall improve long term. The only issue is that it is impossible to advance all the columns at once. Therefore, the base (basic endurance, basic speed, basic force) comes first. Then, the build phase improves muscular endurance and LT capabilities while maintaining the basic skills. The build phase is the most overlooked in my opinion. It seems to the runner that not that much changes while in reality LT development and muscular endurance to make use of the new found basic endurance over longer distances takes more than a couple of weeks time. The prep/race cycle starts out with anaerobic interval runs that will feel bad to horrible at first. But only after a couple of weeks, during which muscular endurance and some base endurance is maintained, all the columns will come together and the entire package of skills will be available to the runner.

My personal experience could not have been more drastic once I changed to this training mantra. The idea of repeating a 10 week 10K plan off the Internet over and over again seamed logical when I started running. It lead to quick improvements during the first months but I soon plateaued. On top of that, tempo runs always felt like all-out races, my heart rate climbed quickly into the anaerobic regime, it was always challenging. The advancement scheme introduced here on the other hand lowered my heart rate significantly during all runs. I hardly ever push my body into the heart rates above 92% of maximum HR any more even during harsh interval runs. The enjoyment of running has improved a lot and my personal best times have improved as well. On top of that, race performance becomes predictable on a whole new level. This is possible, if the entire cycle is completed.

Therefore, even if a marathon is the season highlight and was the goal, it makes not much sense to return to base training right away under all circumstances. If the running took a more endurance running based approach to the marathon he will most likely not have included a lot of interval running into the prep/race cycle. Thus, 1.5K to 5K paces have not been advanced a lot and therefore LT will not advance that much. For these runners, it makes a lot of sense to add a race/prep cycle for a 5K race after the marathon prep/race cycle. Then, the paces in question will be trained, new stimuli are introduced and no pace is neglected. Following this, the new season will begin with a base cycle. LT is maintained at the new found level, easy and endurance pace get the chance to catch up to the new level.

The simple rule of thumb is that easy and LT pace differ by about 60 sec/km if all columns are developed in the right way. The following estimates present a guideline when to progress to the next cycle:

1. Base cycle helps advance easy/endurance paces while LT pace improves insignificantly. Progress to build phase if easy

pace is around 45 sec/km slower than LT pace and/or improvement of easy/endurance pace slows down significantly.
2. Due to high levels of accumulated fatigue, the build cycle does not present a similar rule of thumb. Carrying it out twice should be sufficient for most runners before advancing to the prep/race cycle.
3. Prep/race cycle goals depend on the race. If a marathon is prepared for the cycle is likely so long a maximum of two races fit into one year. After the goal race, a new base cycle is begun. For shorter distance races, a maximum of 8 to 10 weeks are a rule of thumb to advancing race specific paces. Slower races extend this period while faster paces shorten it. A good metric is easy pace. If it slows more than 10-15 sec/km the prep/race cycle is at its end. The runner is now deteriorating his endurance base and will not be able to perform well in fast pace races any longer. A great way to extend the race season is to progress from faster to slower paced races. 5K, then 10K and even a half marathon at the end might carry speed from faster races while focusing on endurance based skills to delay deterioration of base endurance. Ultimately, every runner will have to start anew with the base cycle, just on a new and improved level!

5.4.5 Training plan adjustments

One of the most overlooked aspects of training plans is the need for adjustments as we go. No plan will stand in light of reality. This is a burden to many runners but also an interesting challenge in itself. For the most part of this book, possible changes have already been a vital part of all proposed cycles:

- Downgrading a run by decreasing the training stress (e.g. endurance run to an easy run or an LT run to an endurance run) is efficient to give the body some room for recovery and still providing stimulus for improvement.
- LT runs might be adjusted to LT intervals with one or two

short easy run intermissions of around one minute.
- The number of intervals during interval runs have to be adjusted according to feel.
- Length and intensity of long runs depend highly on weekly running volume and accumulated fatigue across a cycle.
- The final one or two Q-session during a training cycle might be replaced with easy runs if fatigue is all too great.
- An easy run, especially between to Q sessions in across three days might be shortened and/or run below easy pace.
- An entire recovery week might be scheduled if fatigue is already too high after the first or second week of any training cycle (the build phase is a likely candidate).
- taking rest days instead of easy runs

These adjustment all happen at least once during my training year and I am certain they will be needed by many runners. They are key to avoiding injury even under the best possible conditions. If outside influences are added such as harsh work schedules or the common cold they become a means to keep on track for the races to come. The key element is to "live to fight another day" approach meaning that one should not sacrifice future development by focusing on the single workout.

I strongly believe that many injuries can be avoided by listening to what the body tells a runner. These signs can be accumulative and/or acute. The simplest are the acute signs:

- a sharp muscle pain that does not subside immediately during a workout should end the workout right away. A cooldown jog can be attempted but if the pain does remain a walk back is needed.
- Tendon pain during or after workouts can be treated with hot packs (a bean bag does the trick mostly). Yet, if local pain does not subside during warmup the workout could be transformed into an easy run at best. Mostly, it should not be done at all. Riding a bicycle or swimming to maintain basic endurance is a solution instead.

- Strong muscle soreness can occur both as an acute symptom and as accumulated fatigue. The acute version is the muscle pain that is felt during or right after the workout. Muscles have been torn (e.g. during sprints or intervals) though the warmed up state of the body sometimes prevents this from being noticed right away. It depends on the degree of local muscular pain and if the runner is able to maintain the designated workout speed if ending the workout is called for. If pace drops significantly better call it a day which should be obvious if pain becomes too severe.

Accumulated fatigue however is more difficult to assess and needs more experience:

- The progression of any cycle (especially build cycles) is based on the accumulation of fatigue. The body is presented with just too little recovery time so each workout is just a little more taxing. This is because the different systems in the body need different times to recover. If we would always wait for the slowest system to fully recover the body would not improve its ability to run fast. Across any cycle a runner will therefore accumulate muscle tears and some tendon (and other) inflammation. The former is always dealt with with a few recovery days of easy running. The later is harder to detect as no apparent sign is shown. Tendons might hurt at all times but that can be treated like acute fatigue (see above). The real problem to worry about is system wide inflammation which raises resting heart rate. If this metric increases by more than 10bpm extreme caution is required. Often times, motivation to train and decreasing performance in all runs accompanies this phenomenon. The first reflex for many runners is to train even harder which is the worst a runner can do! The body is now in a critical stage with inflammation being or becoming out of control in the entire body. A few days of sub easy running at reduced lengths should show at least some improvement. If not, complete rest and even a visit to the doctor's office is advised. The situation will occur in many runners' training and can mostly be dealt with at the beginning of the problem. I usually feel a lack of motivation to run along with muscle pain much similar to a cold. I then change the run of the day to a sub-easy paced run of around 45min (instead of the usual hour) and a rest day after that. The third day is often another easy run day at which I mostly feel better. A recovery week is the result. For good measure, I add one or two easy running days to make sure the body has recovered enough. What any runner needs to understand is that more training will make the problem worse. Recovery at this point might even elevate the runners' abilities to a new level.

5.4.6 Example of 5K plan including adjustments

In the following, we will look at a prep/race cycle for an example 5K plan and will compare the planned cycle to what was actually trained and how the difference came about. To set a starting point, the base cycle introduced in table 9 with the advancement shown in fig.11 had been carried out prior. After that, two build cycles were carried out, the first following table 12 the second following table 15 to enhance muscular endurance. Following this extensive base and build period, a 5K was attempted. The personal best a year prior of 20:51min (4:10min/km) was to be improved upon. From the advancement of easy and endurance pace the tables by Daniels result in the heart rates and paces in table 41.

Race	-	-	M	HM	10K	5K	3K	1.6K
HR	136	143	158	163	170	175	181	181
Pace [min/km]	5:05	4:53	4:30	4:19	4:08	3:58	3:48	3:34

Table 41: Example Race heart rates and paces [min/km] after base/build cycles.

Easy (5:05min/km) and endurance (4:53min/km) paces were achieved on the comparison run course a few times with better results at the end of the base cycle (4:58min/km and 4:41min/km). Therefore, the set goal of 4:00min/km for the 5K seems realistic. From this starting point, following a recovery week, the 5K plan was begun.

Week 1

Week	Mo.	Tue.	Wed.	Thu.	Fri.	Sat.	Sun.
1	-	8-12x400m @1.5K (3min recovery)	easy 1:00h + 3x8sec sprints	-	5K sub-LT (HM pace)	easy 1:00h	easy 1.5h with 2-3K@10K at the end

- Tuesday: 10x400m between 3:32min/km and 3:42min/km. The last two being the slowest which limited the workout.
- Wednesday: 1h easy run (5:01min/km), no sprints performed
- Friday: 6K sub-LT run (HM-pace) between 4:15min/km and 4:22min/km with a maximum HR of 158, which points towards higher possible performance.
- Saturday: 1h sub-easy run (5:26min/km) because running with a friend.
- Sunday: 1.5h easy run (5:03min/km) with km 11 and 12 being sub-LT (4:17min/km; 4:19min/km)

Comment: It was hard to keep up 1.5K pace during the interval workout because basic speed was neglected during base and build phase (deviating from plan). Also, it felt hard to get into faster pace running after five months of training below 10K pace. Since muscular endurance was a personal issue in the past the sub-LT run on Friday was extended to 6K.

Week 2

Week	Mo.	Tue.	Wed.	Thu.	Fri.	Sat.	Sun.
2	-	5-x800m@3K (3min recovery)	easy 1:00h	-	2x3K LT (HM -10K pace) 2min easy recovery	1x90sec@ 5K 3min recovery at easy pace 1:00h	5K test race

- Tuesday: 5x800m between 3:42min/km and 3:52min/km. The last one was very exhausting due to much head wind.
- Wednesday: 1h easy run (5:08min/km), no sprints performed
- Friday: 3K@LT (4:10-4:14min/km)+ 2K@10K (4:09-4:13min/km) with 1.5min recovery jog. The first 3K were too fast but the second two were still a good performance with maximum HR at 164 on the last kilometer.
- Saturday: 0:45h sub-easy run (5:18min/km) with 1x90sec@4:00min/km.
- Sunday: 5K test race fail (3K between 3:55min/km and 4:08min/km) then break and multiple attempted 4:05min/km segments shorter than 1K. Total of around 5K of high pace running.

Comment: 3K pace seems more doable than 1.5K pace a week before. Another hint that alactic sprints should not be neglected in future base/build cycles. LT run on Friday was more geared towards muscular endurance than LT pace as it was done a little too fast. The higher lactate levels should not be counterproductive since the lactic acid path is not developed at this point. The test race showed all the weaknesses of preparation to this point. The base endurance and raw speed need to be brought together to achieve a good 5K performance. The next LT runs will be run more in the 5K race regime to take the 5K race problems into account.

Week 3

Week	Mo.	Tue.	Wed.	Thu.	Fri.	Sat.	Sun.
3	-	5x800m@ 5K_1minR ccov+1-2x400m@ 3K (3minRecov)	easy 1:00h + 3x8sec sprints	-	5K LT (HM-10K pace)	easy 1:00h	easy 1.5h

- Tuesday: 5x800m between 3:55min/km and 4:00min/km and 2x400m at 3:38min/km and 3:41min/km. Workout was very hard due to 29°C.
- Wednesday: 1h easy run (4:59min/km), 3 sprints performed.
- Friday: Due to failed 5K test race which was because of lacking muscular endurance race paced running was introduced: 5K LT run with 4:15/4:00/4:15/4:00/4:20min/km was planned instead with 4:13/4:00/4:18/4:04/4:19min/km actually done and a maximum HR of 167.
- Saturday: 0:45h sub-easy run (5:47min/km) including some walking.
- Sunday: 1.5h long recovery run with a friend (5:23min/km).

Comment: Despite high temperatures the interval session went rather well. Another hint that basic endurance was achieved but basic speed is lacking. The LT run on Friday had some good performance, much better than the test race at lower heart rates, an improvement is observed. But still, muscular endurance is not sufficient to run a good last kilometer (even though the time was o.k.). The race specific muscular endurance runs with lots of lactate are very exhausting. Thus, the following day is changed to a strict recovery day.

Week 4

Week	Mo.	Tue.	Wed.	Thu.	Fri.	Sat.	Sun.
4	-	5x1K@5K (1-2min recovery easy pace)	easy 1:00h + 3x8sec sprints	-	5K LT (HM-10K pace)	easy 1:00h	-

- Tuesday: 5x1K between 3:57min/km and 4:04min/km and an additional 2x200m at 3:23min/km and 3:46min/km with a max HR of 167.
- Wednesday: 1h easy run (4:52min/km) with a friend that went too fast. Run was almost a progression run with last km 4:34min/km and max HR at 160. Should be classified as endurance run as average HR was 145.
- Friday: Recovery was needed because of Wednesday run too hard. 0:45h easy run (5:04min/km).
- Saturday: 5K tempo run 4:05/4:00/4:00/4:15/4:15min/km was planned instead with 4:07/4:00/4:04/4:14/4:15min/km actually done and a maximum HR of 169. Between km4 and 5 a short break had to be taken due to stomach problems. Overall, a good workout.

Comment: Interval run felt very good, the base endurance helped a lot but the minute of recovery between the intervals is needed due to lack in muscular endurance. Therefore, faster pace intervals were added off plan to stress the muscles out even more. The endurance run on Wednesday was not too fitting for this schedule since to much fatigue was built. Therefore, the LT run had to be moved to Saturday to ensure performance. The tempo run was again within the margins of the revised plan but felt very hard (It also improved 5K PB from the year prior). It seems that muscular endurance is developing throughout the plan. The lactate energy path is also developing as faster running seems much more doable. The prediction at this point is that the goal race pace is possible but that the final kilometer should be very challenging.

Week 5

Week	Mo.	Tue.	Wed.	Thu.	Fri.	Sat.	Sun.
5	-	5x90sec@ 5K 3min recovery at easy pace or Easy	4x90sec@ 5K 3min recovery at easy pace	3x90sec@ 5K 3min recovery at easy pace	-	1x90sec@ 5K 3min recovery at easy pace	5K race

- Tuesday: 0:35h easy run (recovery).
- Wednesday: 1h easy run (5:02min/km) with 4x90sec between 3:59min/km and 4:07min/km. Before the race pace effort legs felt flat, afterward legs felt much better.
- Thursday: 0:50h easy run (4:54min/km) with 3x90sec between 3:49min/km and 3:56min/km. Legs felt very good and speed did not seem to be a problem. Much different to Wednesday!
- Saturday: Again the same as Thursday. Legs felt great and all the muscle soreness is gone now.
- Sunday: Race!

Comment: Tuesday needed to be a recovery day as Saturday was the tempo run day instead of Friday as well as the fact that the tempo run added much more recovery need than initially planned for the LT run. Even on Wednesday this was still observed but the race pace intervals helped. Thursday was on track and was done above planned pace, recovery on Friday is needed as muscles are very sore.

5.5 Alternative Race Cycle for two weeks before race

During most of this book the approach of the final week before a race is to introduce race pace intervals, less and less of them the closer to the race. Although this helps with the preparation of shorter races it might not be the most effective approach for longer ones. The reason is simply that one of the most important aspects of the final two weeks leading to a long race is the recovery from fatigue. A lot of relatively slow running needs to be coped with because volume is key for long race preparation. To recover from this race pace intervals might not be the best answer. For this reason, an alternative approach is simply to to use a number of easy runs with minor variations to remind the body that something different, if only to a small extent, is going to lie ahead.

Mo.	Tue.	Wed.	Thu.	Fri.	Sat.	Sun.
easy 0:30h or rest	easy with 50m elevation delta 0:40h	easy (0:30h) + 1-3 intervals @ race pace effort (1min recovery)	easy with 100m elevation delta 1:00h	easy with drills 0:45h or rest	easy 0:30h	Race

Table 42: Alternative race cycle employing easy running.

Race pace intervals four days prior to a race are quite typical for race cycles. For shorter, faster paced races (say a 1500m race) the entire length of the race will be covered by intervals. E.g. for a 1500m race, this might be two intervals of 800m at 1500m race pace plus one interval of 300m at 800m race pace. For some, even more is possible which depends on the personal level of training. For a mid distance race, between 5K and 10K, it is still possible to use interval length close to race distance (5x1000m for 5K race or 6x1600m for 10K races run at race pace). Yet, for race longer than 10K, the general fatigue of the sheer training volume in the weeks prior is to be recovered from. For these races, it is much more common to only run a couple of longer intervals at race pace, e.g. 3x2000m for a marathon. Which approach an athlete might take depends strongly on how fatigued he is during the day of the scheduled intervals. If he feels fresh he might do a couple, if he is very fatigued he might do one or two and call it a day. The important thing is to prepare for the race and not push too hard to be able to perform a few days later.

5.6 Improvement throughout the cycle

At this point, it is important to discuss the aspect of monitoring progress throughout the training cycle. Again, the example training similar to the approach for the previously discussed 5K will be used. This time, a marathon preparation is the focus.

The following approach was taken to a race that is scheduled in the beginning of May. Therefore, training begins in the beginning of November. Due to a severe cold in September, all training paces are on a somewhat low level which obviously influences improvements (should be more visible improvement than usual for the first 2 months).

The following cycles were used:

- Nov: Base 1 cycle (Fig. 9)
- Dec: Base 2 cycle (speed focus Fig. 10). The cycle only contained the first two weeks, where the third week was a recovery week. The change was made to fill the plan up to race day.
- End of Dec to 1st week of Feb: 6 week half marathon race plan (Fig. 24).
- Rest of Feb: Base 1 cycle (Fig. 9)
- March: Build 1 cycle (Fig. 30)
- 1st three weeks of April: Build 2 cycle (Fig. 31)
- Last week in April and first week in May: Prep/race cycle.

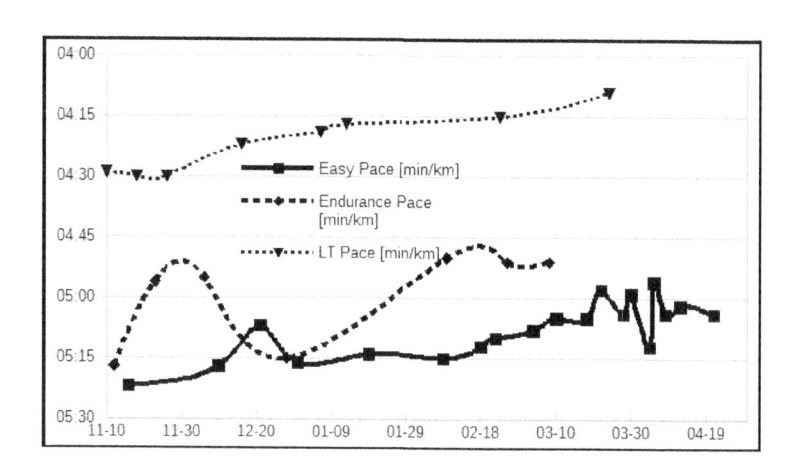

Fig 16: Pace development over time during marathon preparation.

Fig. 16 shows the development of easy, endurance and LT running over the course of the 6 months plan. Due to the specific needs of the marathon race, no standard LT or endurance running could be recorded in the later phases of the plan. Yet, the general progression of running abilities for the three paces is visible.

The first base cycles up until the end of December show a stagnation of LT pace first, endurance pace improved strongly before a sharp decline and easy pace showed an improvement. The reason is that the prior phase of a severe cold had impaired the running abilities a lot. All pace are about 20 sec/km slower than before the infection. This explains some of the inconsistencies.

By the end of the year, this problem was mostly overcome: LT pace is where it was before the cold but easy pace was still a bit slower. The half marathon plan in January focused heavily on muscular endurance. Therefore, improvement in easy pace is there but will not be visible. Fatigue is too strong, keeping up easy pace at this point is sign of improvement alone. The half marathon race in the first week of February felt flat and was below the attempted pace. Yet, the main reason the half marathon cycle was introduced is to prepare the body for some faster long running.

The base cycle that followed for the rest of February then showed the improvement that was implied during the half marathon cycle. Fatigue was reduced and easy running pace improved by about 10sec/km over the course of one month.

The following build cycles showed a further improvement of LT pace to a new level. Yet, a lot of fatigue was introduced through long runs advancing beyond 30km. Therefore, easy and endurance paces appeared to fluctuate. Yet, during the build 2 cycle of marathon preparation, the alternation workout (3km HM pace with 1km easy pace) lead to a new personal best for the half marathon only two days after a 32km long run that contained 18km of endurance pace running. From this development it can be concluded that muscle endurance had improved over the two build cycles as was intended. The half marathon at the beginning of February could at the time only be finished at a pace of around 4:44min/km while HM pace was supposed to be 4:25min/km according to Daniel's tables. A large discrepancy. During the aforementioned interval run it was on the other hand possible to run the fast intervals at a pace of 4:25min/km and the recovery portion at around 4:45min to 5:00min/km, a total of over 22km. This lead to a HM time of under 1h37min which implies that the pace of 4:25min/km could have been attempted under ideal and recovered conditions.

As a result, the progression of the three paces indicates the advancement of the physiological limits of a runner. Yet, they do not provide information about the race specific form. This holds especially true for long races beyond the 5K. If a runner wants to make sure that a certain pace can be achieved during a later race it is wise to introduce this pace again and again into various runs in all cycles. Say, a marathon is planned in an average pace of 4:30min/km in six months time it could be beneficial to add that pace to the end of long runs (instead of LT pace), at the end of LT runs and during fartlek sessions. Even the use of marathon race pace alone in the form of intervals (say 10x1K@M) could be sensible. The reason for this view is that the body will run more efficient at a certain pace if this pace has been run in the past. Up to this point it was implied that the physical abilities of a runner will improve significantly over the course of the entire training plan. But in many cases, the desired race pace is not too far removed from current abilities. Then, race pace can easily be introduced into the plan even into the base cycle.

6. Racing

When it comes to actually running the intended race it strongly depends on the race distance as to what should be done. Obvious, and well mentioned in numerous running books, is that no changes should be made to outfit, shoes, nutrition, etc. on race day. Solid food intake should seize roughly three hours before a race to not upset the stomach too much. All these details are clear to whoever has run races before.

Specific to the race in question is of course the warm up. Any race pace faster than endurance pace requires a warm up, I usually think 15 minutes of easy running should do but e.g. 1500m races might require 30min or more including some drills. What is important is that warm up and race start should ideally be very close together for shorter races as the muscles need to be warmed up enough. For a marathon race, getting the metabolism going is a key element which might mean an earlier warm up is possible or even recommended. The warming up also depends on the absolute pace a runner is going for. For example a pro marathon runner might run the race at 3min/km which requires a thorough warm up compared to a 4:30min/km a great hobby runner might attempt. The bottom line is that any runner needs to find out what works best for them.

Race strategy again depends on what the goal is. In general, to achieve the best possible time in any race, the early and the final kilometer(s) should be a little faster (maybe 5sec/km) than the middle ones in a race. The key is to not overdo the first part to suffer during the second half too much. This especially applies to 5k and 10k races where it is important to have a quick start with the group that runs around the pace an athlete attempts. This often proves difficult as slow runners tend to want to start in the front row. Any time lost on the first kilometer will not be regained during e.g. a 5K race. But also, any power wasted on that kilometer will prevent a good time. Thus, start line positioning and first kilometer pacing is one of the most critical aspects of a great 5K or 10K road race.

For half marathon and especially marathon races this aspect hardly plays a role. 20 seconds lost during the first kilometer do not impact the overall result to such a large extent. Also, in larger events, runners tend to be placed in start blocks surrounded by athletes with similar ability which helps much. The more critical aspect of the first kilometer(s) is to not outpace oneself. Many runners run the first couple of kilometers of a marathon say 15sec/km faster than their attempted average pace for the race. These kilometers will likely hurt them very much. The reason is that any athlete slower than roughly 2:30h has to save as much of his glycogen stores as possible. If your stores last 1.5-2h maximum but the race distance leads to a 3h race glycogen is a precious commodity. The first three kilometers run e.g. at 10K pace might be entirely run in the glycogen consumption regime. The fat metabolism, in the worst case scenario, is not at all developed here and the runner burns off the important fuel at a high rate. For many runners this is the true reason they hit the wall during a marathon. Glycogen stores run out e.g. at kilometer 35 while they would have lasted to kilometer 42 if fuel economy was included into race strategy. Therefore, especially for the first couple of marathons, where the situation is unclear how much sugar the body can take in, the first kilometers might even be attempted 5-10sec/km slower than intended race pace.

The next important issue is fuel consumption. For any race beyond the 10K fuel becomes important for the intermediate runner. Generally, I tend to not drink anything below 1:15h of race time but that is a personal choice. For longer races, especially the marathon, water and sugar consumption is important. Again, pro runners, with marathon times below 2:15h will likely only consume water as the combination of glycogen stores and fat metabolism will get them to the finish line. For intermediate athletes, some sugar substitution is needed. A couple of aspects are important though. First, the body can consume only a limited amount of sugar per hour. This is the first obstacle for many runners. Early in a race they ingest gel package after gel package and get sick later. This is because the gel that exceeds the ability of the body for consumption will sit in the athlete's stomach. Even worse, the water around it will be consumed by the body until a puddle of "glue" forms which will lead to athletes throwing up as the worst case scenario. Second, many runners believe that you can not drink too much water. This is a dangerous attitude as the majority of drinking related collapses of runners a due to too much water ingested not too little. The reason is as simple as it is devastating: the runner's body attempts a defined composition of all body fluids. Heat and exertion result in sweating which offsets this equilibrium. With sweat, electrolytes are excreted. If excessive water is consumed on top of this even more electrolytes are washed out through urination. To an extreme, this can lead to the body simply seizing to function. Runners have died from this mechanism which can easily be prevented. During a race, usually every 5km an aid station is placed in most marathons. I recommend drinking some water during every station. But, at kilometer 5 and 10 stations, half a cup of water is mostly enough. At this point some sugar can be ingested already. A gel with the recommended amount of water or a cup of an electrolyte drink depending on how much sugar an athlete can ingest and what form he prefers. Kilometer 15 is then the assessment period. A foul feeling in the stomach might mean that the sugar sits there. Then, just add water at the next aid stations until the feeling goes away. This might be a cup of water at ever aid station. Clearly, if a runner needs to use the bathroom during a marathon he drank too much. This is a good rule of thumb. If everything goes well, a cup of water with some sugar is taken at every aid station. If a dry feeling in the mouth occurs, more water should be added, maybe a second cup but not bottles of it. At the final aid stations, mixing some coke with water is a great way to getting through the final 5K of a marathon as caffeine is a light stimulant.

 Generally, the question of how much sugar replacement an athlete needs comes to mind. A rough estimate can be done as too much sugar intake will also be a waste. Most running watches show calories burned. This may not be a perfect measurement but an acceptable best guess. Take the number for calories burned for a recent race pace run and extrapolate to race distance (e.g. x calories for a half marathon run at marathon race pace multiplied by two for the marathon race = Y total calories consumed). A certain goal time results for the race, say three and a half hours. Subtract 1.5h (your minimum time of glycogen storage capacity) from your time (3.5h-1.5h = 2h) and divide by total race time (2h/3.5h = 0,57). This gives you an estimate of how much energy needs to be ingested if a runner were to not have any fat metabolism. Multiplied by the energy requirement for the entire race (0,57 x Y = S) results in the alternative need for a calorie source S. Since any intermediate runner will maintain some fat metabolism at marathon race pace this number presents the absolute maximum of sugar needed. A look at the nutritional value information of gels and drinks makes it possible to estimate how much to consume at the maximum. But, this number might exceed the ability of the body to take in sugar. Therefore, the amounts specified can be ingested at kilometer 5 and 10 and the stomach feeling can be assessed. To present an example: at a pace of 4:54min/km an athlete ran a 29km run which was his marathon race pace. His watch tells him he consumed 2600 calories during that run. 2600Calories / 29km x 42.2km = 3780 calories. The marathon time would be 3:27h at that pace. 3:27h - 1.5h = 1:57h. 1:57h / 3:27h = 0.56 and 0.56 x 3780 = 2140 calories. Since a gel package might contain anywhere between 180 and 250 calories one needs around ten gels to substitute all the remaining energy need. This is a little more than 1 gel per 5km aid station. Therefore, if fat metabolism is unknown one gel per 5km aid station for the first couple of stations would be a good plan. If fat metabolism at race pace is known the requirement is obviously reduced. Say, it would be 30% of total energy expended at race pace. Then, we would end up with 3780 x 0.7 = 2650 calories from glycogen which is a significant reduction. Assuming the same 1.5h of glycogen stores (obviously false as the stores now last longer to the tune of 30%) for the sake of the argument only around 1500 calories need to be substituted, only a little over 7 gels which is still the upper limit as glycogen stores are unknown.

What the above discussion shows is that sugar intake needs to be planned for at least roughly for a marathon race while water can always be added for almost immediate substitution. Take into account that the number a runner will calculate with this method will be mostly the (far) upper limit of sugar intake. This means that for example above a runner could very well get away with 5 gels depending on fat metabolism. Therefore, if 1 gel is taken at the first two aid stations and the stomach acts up a little a great race is still possible. But the number of 10 gels should not be exceeded in the above example.

To account for elevated temperatures during a longer race, water

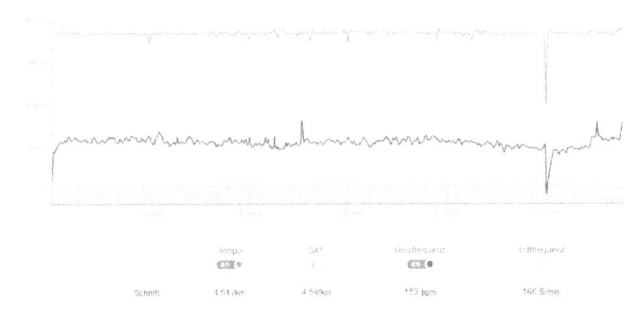

Fig 17: Example for heat influence (+10°C more than normal) in long endurance run (HR elevated).

intake is however the wrong answer. Of course, the body will sweat more, water needs to be substituted. A dry mouth gives a good indication if this is the case. But, the body is best cooled by poring water over head and body. Fig. 17 shows the influence of plus 10°C on the heart rate during a long endurance run. The endurance HR should have been at an average of 144bpm but was found to be at around 152bpm. Every 5 kilometers, excessive water was pored over the entire body to keep the core temperature down. The entire clothing was soaked but the water was almost entirely evaporated at the next aid station. At kilometer 25 a rest stop was needed to drink more than at the other aid stations. Through this method, a further increase in body temperature and heart rate was not observed and the run could be finished at an almost constant pace.

7. Recovery

In the preceding chapters the topic of creating sufficient stimulus to trigger adaptation was covered. It was assumed that whenever a runner does not, or does lightly, train recovery sets in. The recovery then results in supercompensation which in turn leads to increased levels of running ability. These assumptions, although not generally untrue, need to be understood to manage a training plan efficiently. It it necessary to know how recovery works and how insufficient recovery might lead to changes in the training plan at hand. The cycle between following a training plan, recovery and changes to said plan as reaction to a changing reality is what makes training an adaptive cycle. The underlying concept is that even if a training plan takes every aspect of a runner's abilities into account at the starting point of said plan it is impossible to predict the need for recovery down to every detail. For this reason adjustments are a vital part of every plan that often depend on the runner's ability to recover as well as planned.

7.1 Different recovery methods under ordinary conditions

As mentioned before, in theory recovery takes place whenever an athlete does not train. Considering this, it is surprising how little training a runner can take even under the most optimal conditions. This is because the concept of stress and recovery is often times not fully understood. Not the total training load or intensity are responsible for the recovery need. Merely the load and intensity in comparison to what a runner is accustomed to is key. It is of no consequence whether considering a professional athlete training 15 hours per week or the occasional runner training two hours. Both types of runners train, as mentioned before, under a certain regimen they are used to. Training at this regimen requires the recovery the runner is used to while changing it results in changed recovery needs at some point in the future.

The method of recovery but also the timing and duration of it are important to aid to improvement as a runner. In fact, recovery is the most important aspect of a training plan for any runner. The reason for this is that a proper training plan by design exceeds what the given runner is used to. Otherwise there is no training stress and the body sees no need for improvement. Therefore, recovery is always going to exceed the usual amount or methods. In the following section some recovery methods are introduced.

Different runs and different recovery needs

Different training runs naturally imply different needs for recovery. Generally, if one system is tired a different type of training can still be done without impairing recovery. A long easy run might e.g. place little acute stress on muscles, some on tendons and a bit on the metabolic system. A hill LT run on the other hand stresses out muscles among other things acutely while going easy on tendons. Easy and even endurance runs place little acute stress on any system yet help accumulate fatigue over several weeks. One could view fatigue as different categories, one for muscle fatigue, one for impaired resting heart rate and so on. Every training session adds some fatigue to each category with an (personal) upper limit in each one. During total rest the body removes fatigue from each category over time according to personal predisposition. The downside of total rest is that the body often reacts with no or lower improvement or even losses in running ability. With this in mind, spacing of quality session across a training week as well as recovery weeks make much sense. The first aspect is that acute stress needs to be balanced which most often involves muscles and tendons.

A hill LT run places a lot of stress on muscles responsible for lifting the body off the ground. Soreness in the upper legs might be the result. Several days of recovery are needed in return. Yet, the following day, easy running and some alactic sprints are helpful because little stress is put on the same muscles as the day before while other systems are stressed in return. The optimum is to always stress the systems that are not affected much by the last quality session. Key is to know when to take the foot off the gas in the next quality session as it is never possible to train the systems totally isolated from each other. The Friday tempo run of say 6 kilometers might be optimal for one runner, 8 kilometers might be more effective for another. This example is easy to manage: if pace drops significantly during the later stage of the tempo run muscle endurance is mostly responsible. It is also obvious that the hill tempo run on Tuesday may have something to do with it. It is often overlooked that the first kilometers before the drop in pace were effective stress while the drop sets the finish signal. For many other training combinations this relationship is similar only concerning different systems. Thus, acute stress can be managed by understanding which systems are mainly stressed acutely by a training session. The aspect of using the least amount of stress to trigger adaption is key.

More difficult is accumulated stress induced by shear training load. One of the early symptoms of "too much" is diffuse muscle pain in large parts of the legs (in contrast to pain in a specific location). Another indicator would be elevated resting heart rate which points towards inflammation in the cardiovascular system among others. A recovery week would be the first response, total rest if even that makes the condition worse.

In summary, every runner needs to find out how much of which training session is enough for him to trigger adaption while not overly stressing at the same time. In any case, replacing a quality session with some easy or endurance running will most likely do no harm to a designated training goal. In many cases, if only done once in a while, the training goal will more not less likely be reached. Remember, it is always better in the long run to avoid injury and training a little below the optimum.

7.1.1 Short term recovery after every run

The simplest form of recovery a runner has to think about is what to do after any run so effective recovery takes place and what to avoid. Many aspects of discussion in this section have been researched in detail by various scientists. For reference, see "Recovery for performance in sports" by Hausswirth and Mujika.

Recovery drinks:

After every run it is advised to replenish lost fluids with a drink. This far is what most runners are doing already. What many do not know is that the right combination of ingredients aids significantly to recovery especially after high intensity (muscle damaging) runs. Many runners know that sugary drinks help with hydration as water is taken in by the body a lot quicker if sugar (or salt) is added. Also, of course, sugar will help replenish the glycogen stores right away after a run. The first hour after a run the body is more susceptible to quickly replenish the glycogen stores. This window of opportunity should not be wasted. In addition, a certain amount of protein added to the same drink helps the body with immediate muscle damage repair. It is important that the drink is ingested no longer than 45 minutes after a run. In my experience, it is not very important what the individual composition of the drink is. The drink should have a high glycemic index (fast blood sugar increase) and contain a significant amount of protein. I usually mix a standard sports drink (40g of powder with 35g of sugar and 0,7g of salt into 700ml of water) with about 25g of protein powder. In my experience, right about every sports drink available on the market does the trick, also the type of protein seems of limited importance. What is important though is that sufficient protein is ingested to help the body rebuild. Generally, right after a run it is advised to ingest the mixture as early as possible.

Apart from the drink for immediate recovery, sugary drinks should be avoided during rest periods. For hydration purposes I would suggest a 90/10 mixture of water and fruit juice.

7.1.3 Active recovery

Short, sub-easy runs

One of the most effective recovery methods is to schedule a short run at a pace below easy pace. The muscles will have to work a little bit and heart rate will climb somewhat. This helps with blood flow and improves recovery up to a certain point. This point being the severity of fatigue. If, following a training cycle, accumulated fatigue has risen to a point where an additional hard training session seems impossible sub-easy running is very effective. This is the key element of the recovery weeks implemented into the training plans presented in this book. Every couple of weeks it seems effective to reduce training stress and load to give the body room for supercompensation. This method seems more effective than passive rest.

In addition, if acute soreness is present which prevents the athlete from an effective training again sub-easy recovery might be called for.

However, if fatigue becomes too severe, especially after a race, total rest, even for a couple of days is necessary. I usually use sub-easy running, and tend to replace more stressful sessions with it, when I feel I cannot complete the scheduled run but still feel I can run. This implies a balance between the need for recovery and the maintenance of running ability. Sub-easy running is also a good starting point after injury or prolonged post-race recovery.

Easing in after a cold

One important aspect of recovery is getting back into running after a possibly severe cold. Obviously, at one point an athlete wants to get back into running. But also it is known that beginning too early might lead to prolongation of the cold as well as the risk of severe consequences (such as heart muscle inflammation and others). Any runner should be clear that however well he feels there is still a risk of making a cold worse by physical exercise. As with all suggestions in this book, but especially this one, I talk about guidelines and my personal experience much rather than a set of laws. Obviously, any runner should visit a doctor when in doubt. Taking this into account, a rule of thumb is to never run with a fever. If no fever is present, as in the case of a common head cold, I go by feeling. If I (still) feel exhausted I do not train. But sometime during days four to seven mostly after a head cold began I feel like moving again. Then, I schedule a 10 to 20 minute sub-easy run to get my heart rate up and to sweat a little. I monitor my heart rate closely during this run. If it increases beyond what is appropriate for the pace (say 125bpm would be normal for the sub-easy pace and I monitor 140bpm quickly) I walk home and call it a day. This I also do if I still feel too exhausted to continue. This run is basically a test run to assess my current level of recovery (from said cold). The next day is then a rest day followed by an easy run day. If the easy run goes well another rest day follows in my plan and my training is continued as planned after that. Often, I see little reduction of running ability after a cold and the following recovery period. Yet, anaerobic running is probably something to postpone into future weeks to be safe.

7.1.3 Passive Recovery

Stretching

Stretching is probably the one recovery method that has a fixed place in most people's training regime. I used to stretch for many years under the impression that I aided to recovery and injury prevention. Little did I know that no evidence exists for either of these claims. It even seems to be the case that high intensity running leads to micro tears in the muscles. Stretching after such a run pulls the muscle fibers farther apart and even worsens the tears. As a consequence, I have stopped stretching altogether before and after runs. On rest days, I sometime recommend stretching if muscles seem very tight and the needed mobility is impaired. But flexibility exceeding what is really needed for running will on the other hand not support a better running performance. So it seems that stretching has some effect on cramped up muscles but does more harm than good for healthy runners. Therefore, I would not recommend stretching before or after a run.

Compression wear

Compression wear, especially socks, are favored by many runners as a means to increase performance. This claim, however, has also been researched and little evidence has been found in support. Of course, if a runner feels that compression wear helps him perform better he should wear it as also no harm could be found. But apart from a certain mental aspect compression wear seems to only help with recovery. The reason seems to be that blood circulation is improved while resting which in turn improved recovery. In this context compression wear is used by many athletes for recovery while you only tend to see it during races on professional runners who are specifically sponsored by a compression wear company. This should give you some idea how important compression wear is during a race.

Massages (also black roll)

Massages are generally something that is very helpful for recovery. It seems muscles, especially when locally hardened or cramped up, are able to be loosened. Yet, the method seems to have a mainly psychological effect on performance as athletes claim that the massages help them perform better while little if no scientific evidence could be found for improved performance or healing. However, the psychological factor of sports performance is not to be underestimated. Therefore, massage therapy can help athletes perform better through more confidence in their ability to perform (placebo effect). In addition, studies showed a significant improvement in terms of recovery as perceived pain and fatigue was reduced through massage. Especially interesting is the fact that the more experienced the massage therapist was the less pain the athlete felt during the recovery process. This implies that the placebo effect might not be the entire factor present in this case.

Self-massage utilities such as the now popular black roll should have a similar effect. Additionally, the claimed effect on the currently popular fasciae might be called into question. It seems reasonable to assume that in general similar effects as with massages can be achieved. But any additional effects, as often claimed by vendors of the massage rolls, can be called into question.

Rest

Total rest often times implies the reverse question as to how many days a week should be trained on? My rule of thumb is that if a runner is still able to achieve significant improvement in performance, say more than 5sec/km per year across all paces, there is little need to add more training days. This of course from a perspective of somebody who already trains four to five days per week. Giving up rest days often results in injury. A runner should know that as long as fatigue is felt during the entire training cycle at least some stimulus is present. Also, even seven days of rest in a row have been found to not impair running ability too much if sufficient stimulus was present before the period of rest. This is especially true after long races. Many authors recommend one rest day for every 5 to 10 kilometers of race run. I usually recommend two for a 10K race and at least four after a marathon followed by at least one week of recovery running. Taking sufficient rest days after a race usually pays off as the following training cycle can often not be completed otherwise.

7.2 Injury and how prevention works

The topic of pain is generally difficult as pain can indicate any number of things that are wrong. Pain is a very useful indicator that something needs to be changed in your training. Of course the location of the pain is important and also how it started to first appear. The problematic side of pain is that severe as well as benign problems often show similar symptoms. On top of that, any competitive runner will experience pain simply because a fine line exists between useful stress leading towards advancement as a runner and overtraining setting you on a path towards injury.

The rule of thumb is that it is always more productive to train a little below an optimum stress level than to risk injury by going too far. Only a healthy runner is able to advance. But since no runner can pinpoint such a level with accuracy it is advisable to look at different types of pain and how to avoid their occurrence through muscle training.

First of all we are not talking about any sharp pain occurring during a training run or any other workout. The pain important here are two types of pain:
1. muscle or joint pain that seems to be often present especially when not training,
2. joint pain that does subside after warm up.

As a starting point it is often a good idea to find exercises that stabilizes the muscles around the affected area. If pain is present even when not running or after warm up (especially in joints) an acute problem is present that can often not be fixed with a run. In these cases it is necessary to have a doctor assess if permanent damage has been done to e.g. a joint.

First of all, if acute pain occurs during an exercise run stop the run immediately. You might slowly jog back to where you came from if it does not hurt too much. But any farther running will only make matters worse at this point: a sharp pain in a muscle points towards a tear in the muscle which will be torn more if you continue. Even worse, sharp tendon or joint pain might already be a severe injury.

In my opinion one of the most important aspects of the development as a runner is the ability to estimate the state of exhaustion of the runner's own body. Due to running technique and subconscious preferences in feet ground contact certain predispositions for injury exist for every runner. For some it might be a certain tendon for others it is a specific muscle. Fatigue will turn into soreness, it will begin with a pain that fades away after warm up and turn into an always present pain that we would call injury. Normally, injuries do not appear suddenly, unless caused by specific incidents. Thus, the runner needs to pay attention especially to tendon related pain. After warm up, all tendons should ideally be pain free. If not the runner often times has a problem. Some even try to subdue the pain with medication which will only make it worse (never do that!). Any runner needs to understand the art of catching the problem before it turns into an injury. If some specific part of the legs begins to hurt, say a tendon, it needs to be known what can be done short and long term. Massages, heat or cold packs often help, stretching if mobility is impaired or regular muscle training in the area if stability is low. It can even be a systematic problem correlated to bone and muscle alignment. The bottom line is that many sources of information are available to locate the problem. It is an individual journey every runner who wishes to run competitively will have to undertake. If done well, the smallest pain will already be treated as needed by the runner and it will never turn into an injury.

Mobility, the ability to properly move the body, is very important for a runner and in many cases directly related to injuries. Warming up, swinging legs back and forth to get the joints moving is very useful to prevent injury. Especially for older runners these type of exercises are key for staying able to run. For injury prevention, mobility often concerns range of motion. If e.g. the hip can not be extended enough as would be necessary for a proper running motion the knee might have to move out of the way. This might in turn result in knee pain which is really caused by lack of mobility in the hip region (a common problem). I found the book "Ready to run" by Kelly Starrett most helpful to understand causes and possible countermeasures of these indirect injuries.

As the bottom line, I can only recommend designing a sensible training plan that does exceed the current ability (but not by a lot). Then, to introduce exercises stability especially for core stability. Regular mobility exercises aid to prevention of injury. During and after regular training the runner will find out how normal fatigue and soreness feels. Beyond that, the runner has to be aware of anything out of the ordinary. If whatever hurts stays painful or is even getting worse, he should immediately switch into a source finding mode. Where does the pain originate? How can it be treated? Do I need to reduce or change the next training sessions or even switch to cross training or rest? These are the questions to be answered and the effectiveness of the answers will determine if a runner can stay injury free in the long run.

8. Bicycle cross training

Cross training constitutes an important part in any athletes yearly training cycle for which different reasons exist. For one, at the end of a challenging racing season many athletes prefer to cross train for a certain time to ease stress while maintaining their aerobic base. Another reason for the use of cross training very often encountered is the use of cross training to overcome injury or periods of extended fatigue.

In general, many different possibilities of cross training exist. Yet, for the sport of running it is of course advised to use an endurance sport to cross train: cross country skiing, inline skating or cycling are the sports often encountered. In this book, we will focus on cycling as the cross training sport while the same concepts also apply to other endurance sports.

8.1 Heart rate based training

Similar to the running approach introduced above training zones exist for cross training sports as well. Note that these zones are going to be slightly different from the zones applicable for running. This is the reason why fitness tests (lactate and/or breath analysis) for triathletes are separated into two separate tests, one on a treadmill and one on a bike to make the distinction. Among others Joe Fricl ('total heart rate training') offers extensive information about training zones for different endurance sports. For running and cycling a calculator on the web is available (http://www.datacranker.com/heart-rate-zones/). For any given lactate threshold heart rate the differences in training zones occur mostly for the lower end of the spectrum. Easy and endurance heart rates end at lower heart rates for cycling even though the differences are minor.

	Running	Cycling
1 - Active Recovery	0 - 139	0 - 132
2 - Endurance	139 - 145	132 - 145
3 - Tempo	147 - 153	147 - 152
4 - Lactate Threshold	155 - 161	153 - 161
5a - Above Threshold	163 - 166	163 - 166
5b - Aerobic Capacity	168 - 173	168 - 173
5c - Anaerobic Capacity	173 <	173 <

Table 43: Example for heart rate zones for running and cycling (differences yellow) (www.datacranker.com) for LTHR = 163.

Fig. 43 shows heart rate zones for cycling and running for a lactate heart rate of 163. The only substantial difference occurs for recovery and endurance zones but can mostly be overlooked. Yet, individual measurements might reveal much greater difference from athlete to athlete especially concerning the cross training sport. This may have to do with the lack of efficiency in the sport the athlete is less used to. If this is the case then over time the gap should narrow which can be monitored through repeated diagnostics. Another difference that any runner who rarely trains on a bike encounters will be the lack in sufficient muscle development to ride a bike as well as he runs. This results in lower heart rates altogether because muscle fatigue dominates heart rate development. I.e., even at low intensities it is very possible that the ride feels quite hard for the beginner while the heart rate stays within easy or endurance zones. The muscles are not developed well enough to make the higher training zones even possible. Muscles fatigue at comparatively low power while the respiratory system is not even close to its maximum ability. If this phenomenon is the main cause for the difference a runner will see an increase in average power during a fixed heart rate ride following training of the power column. A similar issue can be observed at the end of long endurance races (e.g. a marathon) where heart rate decreases because of muscle fatigue, heart and lunges could go faster but the leg muscles make that impossible.

8.2 Cross training approaches

The aforementioned two goals of cross training in turn result in two main approaches towards cross training: avoiding or reducing fatigue and overcoming injury.

8.2.1 Cross training to overcome fatigue

As mentioned earlier, one of the best stimuli in endurance sports is to increase the number of (especially easy) training sessions per week. This approach is superior to increasing the length of fewer training sessions per week. Yet, if the increase happens too quickly or the athlete is not used to more than a certain number of sessions or training hours per week fatigue and/or injury will be the consequence. If this happens because of e.g. joint and tendon stress cross training should be considered. Even without negative side effects cross training can be used to add a slightly different stimulus.

The most basic use for cross training is e.g. to add additional training sessions on off days to fill the week. An athlete who runs five times per week might then add two easy bike rides on rest days. These easy or even endurance rides should be carried out near optimal cadence (around 90rpm for most athletes).

Mo.	Tue.	Wed.	Thu.	Fri.	Sat.	Sun.
Easy Ride 0.5h	Q1 1h	Easy 1h	Easy Ride 0.5h	Q2 1h	Easy 1h	Q3 long 1.5-2h

Table 44: Example training plan including easy bike rides instead of rest days.

Fig. 44 shows a typical training week and how cycling can be added. Two 30 minute easy rides are added which can be prolonged week after week once the body is used to the new training load. The transition should be rather smooth as the rides aid to recovery and present no additional stress to joint and tendons. The benefit is that blood flow to fatigued muscles, joints and tendons is increased while basic endurance is still trained. Obviously, if fatigue is based on increased resting heart rate, which points towards inflammation of the cardiovascular system, rest days are the better choice followed by easy running (or ride) days. In this case, easy runs could be replaced with easy rides to help with recovery. The distinction can be be made by monitoring resting heart rate and its development over the days. If resting heart rate decreases sufficiently during the night following an easy ride an athlete might consider increasing the length of said rides in the future.

In the case of heavy muscle fatigue and a strength session scheduled in the near future (e.g. hill interval training) the training of the power column can easily be transferred to the bike. A typical training session would be to, after 10 to 15 minutes of warmup, perform cycling intervals at low cadence (around 60-70rpm) and high resistance (e.g. uphill) for two to 10 minutes with easy riding in between. An example session for a seasoned cyclist would be 3 times 10 minutes of high resistance riding with one to three minutes of rest between the sets. For runners who wish to use this type of training the higher end of this spectrum is mostly out of the question. 4 to 7 times 2 minutes of high power riding will do the trick. In theory, the heart rate will approach LT for these workouts but again a runner will most likely not be able to ride with high enough power to affect the cardiovascular system significantly. The result is a very challenging training session with maximum heart rate between endurance and LT heart rates.

Fartleks are also excellent training sessions on the bike. In many training plans, randomly changing paces are often a rare training goal. Yet, in races, changing pace on a hilly course is more often the norm than the exception. Still, it is difficult to add long and/or intensive fartleks into most training plans as they possibly introduce a lot of fatigue as well. A good compromise is presented through the use of cross training fartleks. For cycling, many interval programs exist including varying power and cadence sessions which are really fartleks. Even spinning classes can be used. These fartleks, exhausting as they may be, introduce little tendon or ligament fatigue, you even see these session introduced on the day after a Q interval session of running. Although this might be too stressful for most runners the possibility exists.

On the other hand, speed sessions at high cadence, often a vital part of cycling training plans, are not advised to add to the cross training of a runner. The reason is that the speed column is constituted partly of raw speed, which could be improved on a bike as well, but also partly running economy is trained for. Yet, running economy can best be improved while running, 30 second intervals at 1500m race pace is among the best workouts known in this case.

Mo.	Tue.	Wed.	Thu.	Fri.	Sat.	Sun.
Easy Ride 0.5h	Q1 5x1K@LT pace 1min recovery (1h)	Endurance 6 Hill Sprints (1h)	Easy Ride 0.5h	Q2 25min LT (1h)	Endurance (1h)	Q3 long easy run with 10-20min LT (2h)
Easy Ride 0.5h	Q1 6x1K@10K race pace 1-2min recovery	Power Ride (5x2min high power 60rpm) 0.75h	Easy (1h)	Q2 30min LT (1h)	Easy Ride 0.5h	Q3 long endurance (2h)
Easy Ride 0.5h	Q1 Fartlek (10min LT, 10 min above LT) (1h)	Endurance (1h)	Easy Ride 0.5h	Q2 35min LT (1h)	Endurance (1h)	Q3 long easy run with 10-20min LT (2h)
-	Easy (45min)	Easy Ride 0.5h	Easy (1h)	Easy Ride 0.5h	Recovery (slow) (45min-1h)	long Easy possibly slower (1,5h)

Table 45: Example build cycle including easy bike rides replacing rest days and one power in cycling session to introduce a power stimulus.

Fig. 45 shows a possible adjusted build cycle. Multiple easy rides have replaced rest days while for the training of the power column a run is replaced with a bike ride. This form of adjusting to a given training plan is mainly a fatigue driven adjustment. Whenever the runner feels too fatigued he has the option of adding a rest day. Yet, if cross training is an option, the first step down would be to replace a run with a cycling session. Another reason is that running alone might simply be too boring in the long run. Seven or even more runs per week may be reserved for the professional runner, the obvious choice would be to add cross training to avoid mentally burning out.

8.2.2 Cross training to overcome injury

The second reason why cross training is popular is the management of the healing process after an injury or illness. In the simplest form a common cold may make it impossible to run outside in the winter. Yet, easy to sub-easy running on a treadmill or an equivalent ride on a stationary bike may even aid to recovery. In case of a cold it is of course important that the cardiovascular system and/or the lower respiratory system are not affected. Then, total rest is needed without compromise. But often only the low temperatures outside need to be avoided, a perfect requirement for indoor running or cycling.

When we speak of injury we mostly talk about joint or tendon injuries. Many doctors prescribe total rest which helps with the injury in question but also leads to deterioration of the athlete's endurance base. In this case, what is a healed joint good for if a runner loses two years of basic endurance in the process? It would be far better to heal the joint without the negative side effects.

In many cases, easy cycling (swimming or aqua jogging) is still possible even if running is made impossible by severe injuries. In addition, joints and tendons, which have to be moved in order to increase blood flow, benefit from low impact exercise. Professional athletes, because of their high injury rates, rely heavily on cross training during periods of injury. A professional triathlete even told me that his training partner applied cross training only for the better part of one year due to injury. Even high power interval sessions were part of the training regimen. Surprisingly to many, the athlete in question was not only able to achieve personal bests in cycling after he had recovered but also his running PB improved afterwards. It might therefore even be beneficial to replace most of the runs after the last race of the season (e.g. a two to 4 week cycle) with cycling to give the legs some rest. Another example is the case of another triathlete who was often injured because he was not able to deal with interval sessions on the track. He ended up doing all his training of higher intensity exclusively on the bike while only doing easy and long easy runs (maybe up to endurance pace). This helped him to stay injury free, and because he mainly trained for the ironman distance, had no negative effect otherwise. For short distance running below the 5K race it could be argued that running technique and economy become significant for a personal best. In any case, especially for older runners, being able to avoid high stress intervals may be beneficial for long term development as an athlete. After all, even if cycling has a lower effect than the comparable run, it is still superior to even one injury per year.

Since injuries are individual cases it is not possible to introduce a general concept of how to develop a training plan to overcome them. Yet, examples can be provided that show the general approach which should always be cleared by a physician.

Mo.	Tue.	Wed.	Thu.	Fri.	Sat.	Sun.
injury date	-	-	Easy Ride 0.5h	-	Easy Ride 0.5h	-
Easy Ride 0.75h	-	Easy Ride 0.75h	-	Easy Ride 1h	-	Easy Ride 1h
Easy Ride 1h	-	Easy Ride 1h	Easy Ride 1h	Easy Ride 1h	-	-

Table 46: Example for post-injury training plan.

Fig. 46 shows an example of a post-injury training plan for an assumed injury. Note that injuries are always individual, treatments introduced in this book are suggestions to show basic principles and possibilities. They always involve the risk of making the injury worse and a physician should always be consulted. Let us assume the injury affects the knee which hurts during runs and after. A physician prescribed three weeks of rest. After two rest days swelling is down and walking is possible yet running is out of the question. A runner could then take the risk of trying a slow bike ride to get the legs moving. If this goes well the following day will determine if the injured knee responds well to bike riding. The day after is always an assessment day. If the pain comes back additional rest may be required. This off and on day approach can go on for a couple of days until no discomfort is felt during or after the bike rides. Then, the duration of the bike rides could be increased until one hour of riding is reached. If this still holds up two days in a row and finally three could be introduced as a new stimulus followed by two days of rest to see how the body responds. The trick is to not blindly follow a given plan but to determine if the last stimulus (one day, two or three days in a row) does impair the healing process or not. If it does it might be wise to decrease to the step before (say one day of training followed by a rest day) instead of increasing the stimulus to three days in a row.

This is the part where an athlete needs to listen carefully to his body and adjust the plan on a daily basis. If the changes make it evident that more and more training is acceptable the road seems to lead to recovery. At this point it could be possible to add 30 min of sub-easy running followed by a rest day to try out the theory. In any case, an athlete should not hurry back into a plan and skip over the lost time. This would make matters worse because not only did the runner get injured but he also missed the improvement stimulated by his training plan. It is much better to ease back into a base cycle over the course of a couple of weeks and readjust the upcoming goals altogether.   Cross training at this point will help prevent to loose some fitness, especially basic endurance, but especially race specific fitness will most likely be lost. By returning into running the size of this loss needs to be determined, goals are to be adjusted.

Is the injury present for a longer period of time cross training may be used to maintain the power column as well as basic endurance. Yet, pushing too far will most likely increase the duration of injury which is never beneficial. Therefore, a lot of care needs to be taken.

8. Appendix

Marathon	1/2 Mar	15k LT	12k	10k	8k	5k	3k	1 Mile
84,4%	*88,1%*	*90,2%*	*91,5%*	*92,6%*	*93,7%*	*96,1%*	*99,9%*	*100,0%*
4:56	4:44	4:38	4:35	4:32	4:28	4:21	4:10	3:55
4:45	4:34	4:28	4:24	4:22	4:18	4:11	4:00	3:46
4:35	4:24	4:18	4:15	4:12	4:09	4:02	3:52	3:38
4:26	4:15	4:10	4:07	4:04	4:01	3:54	3:44	3:31
4:17	4:07	4:02	3:59	3:56	3:53	3:46	3:37	3:24
4:09	3:59	3:54	3:51	3:48	3:45	3:39	3:30	3:17
4:02	3:52	3:47	3:44	3:42	3:39	3:33	3:24	3:12
3:55	3:45	3:40	3:38	3:35	3:32	3:26	3:18	3:06

Table 47: First part of pace relationships in min/km and approximate percentage of maximum heart rate.

65,0%	70,0% Easy	73,0% Easy	75,0% Easy	78,1% Endurance	81,3% Endurance	84,4% Marathon
6:22	5:55	5:40	5:31	5:20	5:08	4:56
6:09	5:43	5:29	5:20	5:09	4:57	4:45
5:58	5:32	5:18	5:10	4:58	4:47	4:35

5:46	5:21	5:08	5:00	4:49	4:37	4:26
5:36	5:12	4:59	4:51	4:40	4:28	4:17
5:26	5:02	4:50	4:42	4:31	4:20	4:09
5:17	4:54	4:42	4:34	4:23	4:13	4:02
5:09	4:46	4:34	4:27	4:16	4:05	3:55

Table 48: Second part of pace relationships in min/km and approximate percentage of maximum heart rate.

List of Figures

Fig 1: Example Resting Heart Rate. Head cold on Sat/Sun and following recovery without any training..12

Fig 2: Example of an Easy Run: Heart Rate and Pace development. 25

Fig 3: Example of an Endurance Run - Heart Rate and Pace............26

Fig 4: Exampe of LT run with interruption (warm up and cooldown not shown)...31

Fig 5: Example for LT intervals (5x1K@10K race pace with 1min recovery jog)..31

Fig 6: LT Fartlek (hill, different paces and recovery times)...............32

Fig 7: Example for a Long Run..34

Fig 8: Example for long run @easy HR with LT HR pickup............35

Fig 9: Hill LT run on a housing block circuit....................................38

Fig 10: Example for 4x800m@3K race pace(400m recovery) + 4x400m@1.5K race pace(300m recovery) intervals........................44

Fig 11: Development of Easy, Endurance and LT paces through base cycles..69

Fig 12: Development of Easy, Endurance and LT paces through advanced base cycle...76

Fig 13: Direct (solid) and indirect (transparent) support paces for a 5K example race..95

Fig 14: Progression cycle from general to race specific endurance. 141

Fig 15: Example for athlete's improvement curve over the years...142

Fig 16: Pace development over time during marathon preparation. 163

Fig 17: Example for heat influence (+10°C more than normal) in long endurance run (HR elevated)..170

List of tables

Table 1. Heart Rate Zones (not adjusted)...14

Table 2. Heart Rate zones (adjusted)...14

Table 3. Advised paces for recent 10K race at 45min.......................18

Table 4. Advised paces for recent LT run at 4:20min/km (HR 163bpm)...19

Table 5. My personal steps with several weeks at each step.............59

Table 6. Possible weekly setting for training runs.............................60

Table 7. Final Stage of a weekly training plan..................................62

Table 8. Alternative setup of final stage of a weekly training plan...62

Table 9. Example for monthly progression in the base cycle............66

Table 10: Base cycle with more focus on speed................................71

Table 11: Advanced base cycle with focus on speed and power.......73

Table 12: Example for Build cycle...78

Table 13: Example of build cycle including a Sunday 10K race in

193

week 3..80

Table 14: Example adjustment of pace. 30min LT run can be run comfortably at 4:15. For longer runs, the pace needs to be adjusted accordingly..81

Table 15: Build cycle with focus on muscular endurance.................83

Table 16: Build cycle of example athlete A. Easy pace varies by about 15sec/min..85

Table 17: Prep/race cycle of example athlete B. easy pace varies by about 20sec/min..88

Table 18: Prep/race cycle of example athlete C (Arne Gabius, www.arnegabius.de; Training Arne Gabius). Easy pace varies by about 20sec/min..90

Table 19: Prep Cycles for different race events and 6h weekly running. AE: Anaerobic endurance; S: Speed; E:Endurance column; LT: Lactate threshold..93

Table 20: 5K prep and race cycle(week 5). Note: every run faster than easy pace is preceded by 15min warm up and followed by 15min cool down..98

Table 21: 10K prep and race cycle(week 6). Note: every run faster than easy pace is preceded by 15min warm up and followed by 15min cool down..101

Table 22: Adjusted 10K prep/race cycle following a 5K peak race with muscular endurance constraints..103

Table 23: Half marathon prep/race cycle for a race run at endurance pace. All runs faster than endurance pace include 15min warm up and cool down..106

Table 24: Prep/race cycle for a PB goal half marathon. All runs faster than endurance pace include 15min warm up and cool down.........108

Table 25: Approaches to training cycle design for half marathon races..109

Table 26: Training cycle possibilities for the marathon..................114

Table 27: Endurance based schedule for marathon training............115

Table 28: Build cycle 2 for endurance based marathon preparation (table 27)..117

Table 29: Marathon pace based schedule for marathon training.....120

Table 30: Example of build 1 cycle for marathon preparation at actual marathon pace..121

Table 31: Example of build 2 cycle for marathon preparation at actual marathon pace..122

Table 32: Race cycle for marathon goal event................................123

Table 33: Stepwise approach to reach personal running goal in hours. Monday, some core strength workout can be done and Thursday is rest day..127

Table 34: Hours of training vs. weekly training distribution (easy can also be an endurance run)..133

Table 35: Monthly cycle for an example of 6 hours weekly usual load...135

Table 36: Example time increase for a possible maximum of six hours training per week..135

Table 37: Columns of training emphasized during different training phases..137

Table 38: Skills per training cycle for the example of 6h and 5 sessions of training per week. E=Endurance Column, LT=Lactate Threshold, AE=Anaerobic endurance, P=Power Column, S=Speed

195

Column,..138

Table 39: Adjustment for base cycles design specific to athlete.....145

Table 40: Adjustment for build cycles design specific to athlete....149

Table 41: Example Race heart rates and paces [min/km] after base/build cycles..155

Table 42: Alternative race cycle employing easy running..............161

Table 43: Example for heart rate zones for running and cycling (differences yellow) (www.datacranker.com) for LTHR = 163......182

Table 44: Example training plan including easy bike rides instead of rest days..184

Table 45: Example build cycle including easy bike rides replacing rest days and one power in cycling session to introduce a power stimulus..186

Table 46: Example for post-injury training plan............................188

Table 47: First part of pace relationships in min/km and approximate percentage of maximum heart rate...190

Table 48: Second part of pace relationships in min/km and approximate percentage of maximum heart rate............................191

Printed in Great Britain
by Amazon